How to Carpentry Projects - Building Decks, Trim, Shelves, and Woodwork for the Home

A Comprehensive Guide to Crafting Beautiful Woodwork, Shelves, Trim, and Decks for Your Home

The Fix It Guy

Table of Contents

Introduction

Introduction

Picture this: you're standing in your beautifully renovated home, admiring the custom shelves, trim, and deck that you've crafted with your own hands. The satisfaction and pride you feel are unmatched, knowing that you've transformed your living space into a true reflection of your style and personality. Welcome to the wonderful world of woodworking, my friend!

The Joy of Woodworking

There's something magical about taking a raw piece of wood and shaping it into a functional and beautiful object. The process of woodworking is not only rewarding but also therapeutic. As you focus on each cut, sand, and finish, you'll find yourself lost in the moment, your worries and stress melting away. The scent of freshly cut wood, the feel of the grain beneath your fingers, and the sound of tools shaping the material – it's a sensory experience like no other.

Benefits of DIY Carpentry Projects

Not only is woodworking a fun and engaging hobby, but it also comes with a host of benefits. When you take on a DIY carpentry project, you're not just creating something beautiful – you're also saving money. Imagine the cost of hiring a professional to build custom shelves or install trim in your home. By doing it yourself, you'll save a significant amount of money that you can put towards other home improvements or simply enjoy as extra savings.

But the benefits don't stop there. When you build something with your own hands, you'll feel a sense of accomplishment and pride that can't be matched. You'll be able to look at your creations every day, knowing that you put in the time, effort, and skill to bring them to life. Plus, you'll be learning valuable skills that you can use for a lifetime, and even pass down to future generations.

Essential Tools and Materials

Now, I know what you might be thinking – "I don't have the tools or skills to take on a woodworking project!" But fear not, my friend. With a few essential tools and materials, you'll be well on your way to crafting beautiful pieces for your home. In this book, we'll cover everything you need to get started, from basic hand tools like saws and hammers to power tools like drills and sanders. We'll also discuss the different types of wood and materials you can use, and how to choose the right ones for your project.

But tools and materials are just the beginning. Throughout this book, we'll guide you through the entire process of woodworking, from planning and designing your project to executing each step with precision and care. We'll cover safety tips to keep you protected while you work, and provide troubleshooting advice for when things don't go quite as planned.

Whether you're a beginner looking to take on your first project, or an experienced woodworker looking to expand your skills, this book has something for everyone. So dive in, get ready to create, and let's build something beautiful together!

Chapter 1
Safety First
Proper Use of Personal Protective Equipment

When it comes to woodworking, safety should always be your top priority. No matter how excited you are to start your project, taking the time to properly use personal protective equipment (PPE) is essential to prevent injuries and ensure a enjoyable, stress-free woodworking experience. In this chapter, we'll dive deep into the proper use of PPE, so you can confidently and safely tackle any carpentry project.

1. Eye Protection

Your eyes are one of your most valuable assets, and protecting them should be a non-negotiable part of your woodworking routine. Always wear safety glasses or goggles that are impact-resistant and provide clear, unobstructed vision. Make sure your eye protection fits comfortably and securely, and don't be tempted to remove it, even for a moment.

When selecting eye protection, consider the specific tasks you'll be undertaking. For example, if you'll be doing a lot of sanding, choose glasses or goggles with additional side shields to protect against dust and debris. If you'll be working with chemicals or stains, opt for goggles that provide a tight seal around your eyes to prevent splashes or fumes from entering.

2. Hearing Protection

Many woodworking tools, such as saws and routers, produce high levels of noise that can cause permanent hearing damage over time. To protect your ears, always wear hearing protection when operating loud machinery. There are two main types of hearing protection: earplugs and earmuffs.

Earplugs are small, foam inserts that fit directly into your ear canal. They're lightweight, comfortable, and easy to carry around, making them a popular choice for many woodworkers. However, they may not provide as much protection as earmuffs, and they can be tricky to insert correctly.

Earmuffs, on the other hand, fit over your entire ear and provide a higher level of noise reduction. They're a good choice for extended woodworking sessions or when working with particularly loud tools. However, they can be bulky and hot, and some people find them less comfortable than earplugs.

When selecting hearing protection, look for products with a high Noise Reduction Rating (NRR). The higher the NRR, the more protection the device provides. If you'll be using both earplugs and earmuffs together, make sure they're compatible and don't interfere with each other's fit.

3. Respiratory Protection
Woodworking generates a lot of dust, which can be harmful to your lungs if inhaled. To protect your respiratory system, always wear a dust mask or respirator when sanding, sawing, or working with any materials that create fine particles.

Dust masks are lightweight, disposable masks that cover your nose and mouth. They're effective at filtering out larger dust particles, but may not provide adequate protection against finer particles or fumes. Respirators, on the other hand, are more heavy-duty and can filter out both large and small particles, as well as fumes and vapors.

When selecting a dust mask or respirator, choose one that fits snugly against your face, with no gaps or leaks. Make sure it's rated for the specific type of dust or fumes you'll be encountering, and replace the filters or cartridges as needed.

4. Hand Protection

Your hands are your most important tools when it comes to woodworking, so protecting them is crucial. Always wear gloves when handling rough or splintery wood, or when working with sharp tools or blades.

Leather gloves are a popular choice for woodworkers, as they provide good grip and protection against cuts and abrasions. However, they can be bulky and may limit your dexterity for more delicate tasks. Nitrile or latex gloves are a good alternative for tasks that require more precision, as they provide a snug fit and good tactile sensitivity.

When selecting gloves, choose a pair that fits well and allows for easy movement of your fingers. Avoid gloves that are too loose or too tight, as they can interfere with your grip or dexterity.

5. Footwear

Protecting your feet is just as important as protecting your hands and eyes. Always wear sturdy, closed-toe shoes when working in your workshop. Steel-toed boots are a good choice for heavy-duty projects or when working with large, heavy materials.

In addition to protecting your feet from falling objects, proper footwear can also help prevent slips and falls. Look for shoes with good traction and support, and avoid wearing sandals, flip-flops, or other open-toed shoes in the workshop.

By properly using personal protective equipment, you can minimize the risk of injuries and ensure a safe, enjoyable woodworking experience. Remember, safety should always come first – no project is worth risking your health or well-being. Take the time to invest in high-quality PPE, and make a habit of wearing it every time you enter your workshop. Your future self will thank you!

Maintaining a Safe Work Environment

In addition to using personal protective equipment, maintaining a safe work environment is essential for preventing accidents and injuries in your workshop. A well-organized, clean, and properly equipped workspace not only enhances your safety but also makes your woodworking experience more enjoyable and efficient. In this section, we'll explore the key aspects of maintaining a safe work environment.

1. Workshop Layout and Organization

The layout and organization of your workshop play a crucial role in maintaining a safe work environment. A cluttered, disorganized space can lead to accidents, as well as decreased productivity and enjoyment.

Start by assessing your workspace and removing any unnecessary items or debris. Make sure you have plenty of clear, unobstructed areas for working, as well as designated spaces for storing tools, materials, and equipment. Use shelves, cabinets, and pegboards to keep your tools and supplies organized and easily accessible.

When arranging your workshop, consider the flow of your work process. Place frequently used tools and equipment within easy reach, and make sure there's enough space to move around comfortably. Avoid placing tools or materials in high-traffic areas or near doorways, where they could create tripping hazards.

2. Proper Lighting

Good lighting is essential for maintaining a safe work environment. Inadequate or harsh lighting can cause eye strain, fatigue, and even accidents, as it can make it difficult to see potential hazards or read tool markings accurately.

Make sure your workshop has plenty of bright, even lighting, especially in areas where you'll be doing detailed work or operating power tools. Natural light is ideal, so if possible, position your workspace near windows or skylights. If you're relying on artificial light, choose fixtures that provide a balanced, glare-free illumination, such as adjustable task lights or overhead fluorescent bulbs with diffusers.

In addition to general lighting, consider adding task-specific lighting for certain tools or workstations. For example, a flexible, adjustable light can be helpful when working with a drill press or bandsaw, while a magnifying lamp can make it easier to see small details when doing intricate work.

3. Electrical Safety
Many woodworking tools and equipment rely on electricity, so electrical safety is a critical component of maintaining a safe work environment. Improper use or maintenance of electrical equipment can lead to fires, shocks, or other serious accidents.

Start by making sure all of your electrical equipment is properly grounded and in good working condition. Regularly inspect cords and plugs for signs of wear or damage, and replace them as needed. Avoid running cords across walkways or under rugs, where they can be damaged or create tripping hazards.

When working with power tools, always use outlets that are protected by ground fault circuit interrupters (GFCIs). These devices can help prevent shocks and electrocution by quickly cutting off power if they detect an imbalance in the electrical current.

If you're not comfortable working with electricity, don't hesitate to hire a professional electrician to install or repair electrical equipment in your workshop. It's better to err on the side of caution than to risk injury or damage.

4. Fire Safety

Woodworking involves many materials and processes that can create fire hazards, such as sawdust, wood shavings, and flammable finishes. To maintain a safe work environment, it's essential to take steps to prevent and prepare for potential fires.

Start by keeping your workshop clean and free of debris. Regularly sweep or vacuum up sawdust and wood shavings, and dispose of them in a metal container with a tight-fitting lid. Avoid letting dust accumulate on surfaces or in corners, where it can easily ignite.

When working with flammable liquids, such as finishes or solvents, make sure to store them in approved containers and keep them away from heat sources or sparks. Use these products in a well-ventilated area, and avoid smoking or using open flames nearby.

In case of a fire, make sure your workshop is equipped with appropriate fire extinguishers and that you know how to use them. Keep extinguishers in easily accessible locations, and make sure they're properly charged and maintained. It's also a good idea to have a fire escape plan in place and to practice it regularly, so you know what to do in case of an emergency.

5. Tool Maintenance and Storage

Properly maintaining and storing your tools is another important aspect of maintaining a safe work environment. Dull, damaged, or improperly adjusted tools can create safety hazards, as well as produce poor-quality results.

Regularly inspect your tools for signs of wear or damage, and repair or replace them as needed. Keep blades sharp and clean, and make sure all guards and safety features are in place and functioning properly. Follow the manufacturer's instructions for adjusting and maintaining each tool, and don't hesitate to seek professional help if you're unsure how to proceed.

When storing tools, make sure they're secure and protected from damage. Use tool chests, cabinets, or racks to keep them organized and easily accessible. Avoid leaving tools out on workbenches or floors, where they can be knocked over or create tripping hazards.

By taking the time to maintain a safe work environment, you can prevent accidents, reduce the risk of injury, and make your woodworking experience more enjoyable and productive. Remember, a safe workshop is a happy workshop – so make safety a priority in all of your carpentry projects!

Handling Tools and Materials Safely

Proper handling of tools and materials is crucial for maintaining a safe and efficient woodworking environment. By understanding the potential hazards associated with each tool and material, and following best practices for safe handling, you can minimize the risk of accidents and ensure the success of your projects. In this section, we'll delve into the key principles of handling tools and materials safely.

1. Read and Follow Manufacturer's Instructions

Before using any new tool or material, always take the time to read the manufacturer's instructions and safety guidelines. These resources provide valuable information on the proper use, maintenance, and storage of the item, as well as any potential hazards or precautions to be aware of.

Pay close attention to the recommended safety equipment, such as eye protection or dust masks, and make sure to use them as directed. If you have any questions or concerns about the proper use of a tool or material, don't hesitate to reach out to the manufacturer or consult with a more experienced woodworker.

2. Inspect Tools Before Use

Before each use, take a moment to inspect your tools for any signs of damage, wear, or malfunction. Check for cracks, chips, or dents in the body of the tool, as well as any loose or missing parts. Make sure all guards, handles, and safety features are securely attached and functioning properly.

If you notice any issues, don't attempt to use the tool until it has been repaired or replaced. Using a damaged or malfunctioning tool can lead to accidents, injuries, or poor-quality results.

3. Use the Right Tool for the Job

One of the most important principles of safe tool handling is to always use the right tool for the job at hand. Attempting to use a tool for a purpose it wasn't designed for can lead to accidents, damage to the tool or workpiece, or poor results.

For example, using a screwdriver as a chisel or pry bar can cause the tip to break off and become a projectile hazard. Similarly, using a dull or improperly sized saw blade can cause the blade to bind or kick back, potentially causing injury to the operator.

Before starting a project, take the time to assess the tools and materials you'll need, and make sure you have the appropriate items on hand. If you're unsure which tool to use for a particular task, consult with a more experienced woodworker or refer to reliable resources, such as woodworking books or online forums.

4. Maintain a Clean and Organized Work Area

A cluttered, disorganized work area can create numerous hazards when handling tools and materials. Loose debris, such as sawdust or wood scraps, can create slipping or tripping hazards, while misplaced tools or materials can lead to accidents or delays in your work.

To maintain a safe and efficient workspace, make a habit of regularly cleaning and organizing your area. Sweep or vacuum up sawdust and debris after each work session, and dispose of them properly. Keep your tools and materials neatly organized and easily accessible, using tool chests, shelves, or pegboards as needed.

In addition to preventing accidents, a clean and organized work area can also help you work more efficiently and enjoyably. When everything is in its place and easily accessible, you can focus on the task at hand without wasting time searching for misplaced items.

5. Use Clamps and Vises for Stability
When working with power tools or hand tools, it's important to keep your workpiece stable and secure. Attempting to hold a workpiece with one hand while operating a tool with the other can lead to slips, inaccurate cuts, or other accidents.

To ensure stability and safety, always use clamps, vises, or other workholding devices to secure your workpiece before beginning to cut or shape it. Make sure the clamps are tightened securely and positioned in a way that won't interfere with the tool or the cut.

In addition to preventing accidents, using clamps and vises can also help you achieve more accurate and precise results. By eliminating movement or vibration in the workpiece, you can create cleaner, more consistent cuts and shapes.

6. Handle Materials with Care
In addition to tools, it's important to handle materials safely and carefully. Many common woodworking materials, such as lumber or sheet goods, can be heavy, awkward, or prone to splintering or breaking if handled improperly.

When handling large or heavy materials, always use proper lifting techniques to avoid strain or injury. Bend at the knees, keep your back straight, and lift with your legs, not your back. If a piece is too heavy or awkward to lift alone, ask for assistance or use a mechanical aid, such as a dolly or hand truck.

When cutting or shaping materials, be aware of the potential for kickback or binding. Use push sticks, featherboards, or other safety devices to keep your hands away from the blade or cutter, and always feed the material in the proper direction to minimize the risk of kickback.

7. Store Tools and Materials Properly

Proper storage of tools and materials is essential for maintaining a safe and organized woodworking environment. When tools and materials are left out or stored haphazardly, they can create tripping hazards, become damaged or dull, or even pose fire or chemical hazards.

To store tools safely, use designated storage areas, such as tool chests, cabinets, or racks. Make sure each tool has a specific place to be stored, and always return it to that place when not in use. Regularly inspect your storage areas for any signs of damage, wear, or moisture, and address any issues promptly.

When storing materials, such as lumber or sheet goods, make sure they are stacked securely and evenly to prevent tipping or collapsing. Use lumber racks or shelves to keep materials off the ground and away from moisture or pests. If storing flammable or combustible materials, such as finishes or solvents, make sure to use approved containers and store them in a cool, dry, well-ventilated area away from heat sources or sparks.

By following these principles for handling tools and materials safely, you can create a safer, more efficient, and more enjoyable woodworking environment. Remember, the key to success is to always prioritize safety, take the time to properly use and maintain your tools and materials, and never hesitate to ask for help or guidance when needed. With a commitment to safe practices, you can unlock your full potential as a woodworker and create beautiful, lasting projects for years to come.

Chapter 2
Mastering the Basics
Understanding Wood Types and Properties

To create successful woodworking projects, it's essential to have a solid understanding of the basics. One of the most fundamental aspects of woodworking is understanding the different types of wood and their properties. By learning about the characteristics, strengths, and limitations of various wood species, you can make informed decisions about which materials to use for your projects, and how to work with them effectively. In this section, we'll take an in-depth look at understanding wood types and properties.

Understanding Wood Types and Properties

1. Hardwoods vs. Softwoods

Wood is generally classified into two main categories: hardwoods and softwoods. Despite what their names might suggest, these categories don't necessarily refer to the actual hardness or density of the wood, but rather to the type of tree from which the wood is harvested.

Hardwoods come from deciduous trees, which are trees that lose their leaves annually. Examples of hardwoods include oak, maple, cherry, walnut, and mahogany. Hardwoods are typically denser, more durable, and more resistant to wear and tear than softwoods. They also tend to have a more complex grain pattern and a wider range of colors and textures, making them popular choices for furniture, cabinetry, and decorative projects.

Softwoods, on the other hand, come from coniferous trees, which are trees that bear cones and have needles instead of leaves. Examples of softwoods include pine, cedar, spruce, and fir. Softwoods are typically lighter, less dense, and more affordable than hardwoods. They are often used for construction lumber, framing, and utility projects, as well as for some furniture and decorative applications.

2. Grain Patterns and Texture

Another important aspect of understanding wood types is recognizing the different grain patterns and textures that each species can exhibit. The grain pattern refers to the arrangement and alignment of the wood fibers, while the texture refers to the tactile feel of the wood surface.

Some common grain patterns include:

- Straight grain: A uniform, parallel alignment of the wood fibers, creating a smooth, consistent appearance.
- Wavy grain: A undulating, irregular alignment of the wood fibers, creating a flowing, decorative effect.
- Curly grain: A series of small, tight waves or ripples in the wood fibers, creating a shimmering, three-dimensional appearance.
- Burled grain: A swirling, knotted arrangement of the wood fibers, creating a highly figured, decorative pattern.

The texture of the wood can also vary widely between species, ranging from fine and smooth to coarse and rough. Some woods, such as cherry or maple, have a very fine, even texture that is well-suited for intricate carving or turning. Others, such as oak or ash, have a more pronounced, open-grained texture that can add visual interest and depth to a project.

3. Dimensional Stability and Movement

Wood is a hygroscopic material, meaning that it absorbs and releases moisture from the surrounding environment. As a result, wood can expand, contract, or warp as its moisture content changes. This phenomenon is known as wood movement, and it's an important consideration when planning and executing woodworking projects.

Different wood species have different levels of dimensional stability, or resistance to movement. Some woods, such as cedar or redwood, are naturally resistant to moisture and decay, making them good choices for outdoor projects or humid environments. Others, such as basswood or butternut, are more prone to movement and require careful acclimation and storage to prevent warping or cracking.

To minimize the effects of wood movement, it's important to allow your wood to acclimate to your workshop environment before beginning a project. This means storing the wood in the same space where it will be used, and allowing it to adjust to the ambient temperature and humidity levels. It's also important to design your projects with wood movement in mind, using techniques such as floating panels, expansion gaps, or breadboard ends to allow for seasonal changes in size and shape.

4. Workability and Machinability

Different wood species also have different levels of workability and machinability, which refer to how easily the wood can be cut, shaped, and finished using various tools and techniques. Some woods, such as basswood or pine, are relatively soft and easy to work with hand tools or power tools. Others, such as hard maple or purpleheart, are much denser and more challenging to cut or shape, requiring sharp blades and more powerful equipment.

The workability of a wood can also be affected by its grain pattern and texture. Woods with straight, even grain are generally easier to cut and shape than those with irregular or figured grain. Similarly, woods with a fine, uniform texture are often easier to sand and finish than those with a coarse or open-grained texture.

When selecting a wood for a project, it's important to consider its workability and machinability in relation to your skill level, available tools, and desired outcomes. If you're a beginner, it may be best to start with a softer, more forgiving wood like pine or poplar, and work your way up to more challenging species as you gain experience and confidence.

5. Color and Appearance
One of the most striking aspects of different wood species is their wide range of colors and visual characteristics. From the creamy white of holly to the deep, rich browns of walnut, the color of the wood can have a significant impact on the overall look and feel of a project.

In addition to the base color, many woods also exhibit unique visual features such as knots, burls, or mineral streaks. These characteristics can add depth, character, and individuality to a piece, but they can also pose challenges in terms of workability or consistency.

When selecting a wood for a project, it's important to consider the desired color and appearance, as well as any potential variations or imperfections that may be present. Some woods, such as cherry or oak, will naturally darken or change color over time due to exposure to light and air. Others, such as maple or ash, can be stained or dyed to achieve a specific color or effect.

6. Cost and Availability

Finally, it's important to consider the cost and availability of different wood species when planning a project. Some woods, such as pine or oak, are readily available and relatively affordable, making them good choices for budget-conscious projects or large-scale applications. Others, such as exotic hardwoods or figured veneers, can be much more expensive and harder to source, limiting their use to smaller, more specialized projects.

When selecting a wood for a project, it's important to balance your desired characteristics and aesthetics with your available budget and resources. In some cases, it may be possible to achieve a similar look or effect using a more affordable or accessible wood species, or by using techniques such as staining, painting, or veneering.

By understanding the different types of wood and their properties, you can make informed decisions about which materials to use for your projects, and how to work with them effectively. Whether you're a beginner or an experienced woodworker, taking the time to learn about the characteristics, strengths, and limitations of various wood species can help you create successful, beautiful projects that showcase the natural beauty and versatility of this remarkable material.

Measuring and Marking Techniques

Accurate measuring and marking are essential skills for any woodworker. Whether you're cutting lumber to size, laying out joinery, or creating intricate designs, the ability to measure and mark precisely can make the difference between a successful project and a frustrating one. In this section, we'll explore the various tools and techniques used for measuring and marking in woodworking.

1. Measuring Tools

There are several essential measuring tools that every woodworker should have in their toolkit. These include:

a. Tape Measure: A retractable metal or fiberglass tape with linear measurements, typically ranging from 12 to 100 feet in length. Tape measures are versatile and convenient for measuring longer distances or larger pieces of lumber.

b. Folding Rule: A compact, foldable ruler made of wood or plastic, typically 6 or 8 feet in length. Folding rules are handy for measuring shorter distances or in tight spaces where a tape measure may be cumbersome.

c. Combination Square: A multi-purpose measuring and marking tool consisting of a metal ruler and a sliding head with a 90-degree angle. Combination squares are used for measuring, marking right angles, and checking the squareness of edges or corners.

d. Marking Gauge: A tool consisting of a beam with a sliding head and a sharpened pin or blade, used for marking consistent parallel lines or setting out joinery.

e. Calipers: A tool consisting of two curved arms joined at a hinge, used for measuring the thickness, diameter, or depth of an object. Calipers can be either analog or digital and are particularly useful for measuring irregular or curved surfaces.

2. Marking Tools

In addition to measuring tools, there are several essential marking tools that are used in woodworking. These include:

a. Pencil: A traditional graphite pencil is the most basic and versatile marking tool in woodworking. Pencils are easy to use, easy to erase, and provide a clear, visible line.

b. Marking Knife: A sharp, pointed blade used for making precise, clean lines in the wood. Marking knives are particularly useful for marking joinery or creating crisp, accurate lines for sawing or chiseling.

c. Awl: A sharp, pointed tool used for making small indentations or holes in the wood. Awls are often used for marking the location of screws, nails, or dowels.

d. Chalk Line: A tool consisting of a string coated with chalk dust, used for marking long, straight lines on larger pieces of lumber or sheet goods. Chalk lines are particularly useful for breaking down larger pieces into smaller, more manageable sizes.

3. Measuring Techniques

Accurate measuring is essential for ensuring that your project turns out as planned. Here are some key techniques for measuring effectively:

a. Use the Right Tool for the Job: Select the appropriate measuring tool based on the size and scale of your project. For example, use a tape measure for longer distances, a combination square for shorter distances and right angles, and calipers for measuring thickness or diameter.

b. Measure Twice, Cut Once: Always double-check your measurements before making a cut. This helps to prevent costly mistakes and ensures that your pieces will fit together properly.

c. Use Benchmarks and Reference Points: When measuring longer distances or multiple pieces, use benchmarks or reference points to ensure consistency and accuracy. For example, use a story stick or a set of dividers to transfer measurements from one piece to another.

d. Account for Blade Thickness: When measuring for cuts, always account for the thickness of your saw blade or cutting tool. This is known as the "kerf" and can vary depending on the type and size of the blade.

e. Use Relative Dimensioning: Instead of relying solely on absolute measurements, use relative dimensioning whenever possible. This means measuring and marking based on the actual size and shape of your workpiece, rather than an arbitrary set of numbers.

4. Marking Techniques

Accurate marking is just as important as accurate measuring in woodworking. Here are some key techniques for marking effectively:

a. Use a Sharp Pencil or Knife: A sharp pencil or marking knife will create a clean, precise line that is easy to follow when cutting or shaping your workpiece. Avoid using dull or blunt marking tools, as these can create fuzzy or inaccurate lines.

b. Mark on the Waste Side: When marking for cuts, always mark on the waste side of your line. This means that your marked line will be removed when you make your cut, leaving a clean, accurate edge on your workpiece.

c. Use a Marking Gauge for Consistent Lines: When marking parallel lines or setting out joinery, use a marking gauge to ensure consistency and accuracy. A marking gauge allows you to set a fixed distance from the edge of your workpiece and create a clean, straight line.

d. Use a Square for Perpendicular Lines: When marking perpendicular lines or checking for square, use a combination square or try square. These tools have a built-in 90-degree angle that ensures your lines will be perfectly perpendicular to the edge of your workpiece.

e. Use Centerlines and Datum Points: When marking complex shapes or joinery, use centerlines and datum points to establish a clear, consistent reference. This helps to ensure that your pieces will align properly and that your joinery will be accurate and strong.

5. Best Practices for Measuring and Marking
To ensure the best results in your woodworking projects, follow these best practices for measuring and marking:

a. Keep Your Tools in Good Condition: Regularly inspect and maintain your measuring and marking tools to ensure that they are accurate and in good working order. Clean and oil your tools as needed, and replace any damaged or worn parts.

b. Work on a Flat, Stable Surface: When measuring and marking, always work on a flat, stable surface such as a workbench or assembly table. This helps to ensure that your measurements and markings will be accurate and consistent.

c. Use Clamps or Stops to Secure Your Work: When measuring or marking longer pieces or multiple pieces, use clamps or stops to secure your work in place. This helps to prevent movement or shifting and ensures that your measurements and markings will be accurate.

d. Take Your Time and Be Patient: Measuring and marking can be tedious and time-consuming, but it's important to take your time and be patient. Rushing through the process can lead to mistakes or inaccuracies that can affect the entire project.

e. Double-Check Your Work: Before making any cuts or moving on to the next step, always double-check your measurements and markings to ensure that they are accurate and complete. This helps to catch any mistakes early and prevents costly errors down the line.

By mastering these measuring and marking techniques and following these best practices, you can ensure that your woodworking projects will be accurate, precise, and successful. Whether you're a beginner or an experienced woodworker, taking the time to measure and mark carefully is an essential part of the craft, and a skill that will serve you well in all your future projects.

Cutting and Shaping Wood

Cutting and shaping wood are fundamental skills in woodworking that allow you to transform raw lumber into the precise pieces needed for your projects. Whether you're using hand tools or power tools, the ability to cut and shape wood accurately and efficiently is essential for creating strong, beautiful, and functional pieces. In this section, we'll explore the various tools and techniques used for cutting and shaping wood.

1. Hand Tools for Cutting

There are several essential hand tools used for cutting wood, each with its own specific purpose and technique. These include:

a. Hand Saw: A traditional tool consisting of a toothed blade attached to a handle, used for making straight cuts in wood. There are many different types of hand saws, including rip saws, crosscut saws, and backless saws, each designed for a specific type of cut.

b. Coping Saw: A small, thin-bladed saw used for making intricate or curved cuts in wood. Coping saws have a narrow, flexible blade that can be easily maneuvered to follow a template or pattern.

c. Chisel: A sharp, flat-edged tool used for cutting, shaping, and removing small amounts of wood. Chisels come in various sizes and shapes, each designed for a specific task, such as paring, chopping, or mortising.

d. Drawknife: A traditional tool consisting of a sharp, curved blade with handles on each end, used for shaving and shaping wood. Drawknives are particularly useful for creating round or curved shapes, such as chair legs or tool handles.

2. Power Tools for Cutting

In addition to hand tools, there are several power tools commonly used for cutting wood. These tools offer greater speed, efficiency, and precision than hand tools, but also require proper safety precautions and technique. Some common power tools for cutting include:

a. Circular Saw: A handheld power saw with a circular blade, used for making straight cuts in wood. Circular saws are versatile and portable, making them a popular choice for jobsite work and home projects.

b. Table Saw: A stationary power saw with a circular blade mounted beneath a flat table, used for making precise, repeatable cuts in wood. Table saws are a foundational tool in most woodworking shops and are used for ripping, crosscutting, and making angled cuts.

c. Miter Saw: A power saw with a circular blade mounted on a pivoting arm, used for making accurate crosscuts and angled cuts in wood. Miter saws are particularly useful for cutting trim, molding, and picture frames.

d. Band Saw: A stationary power saw with a continuous loop of toothed metal blade, used for making curved or irregular cuts in wood. Band saws are versatile tools that can be used for ripping, resawing, and cutting complex shapes.

3. Cutting Techniques

Regardless of whether you're using hand tools or power tools, there are several key techniques for cutting wood safely and accurately. These include:

a. Proper Blade Selection: Choose the appropriate blade for the type of cut you're making and the material you're cutting. For example, use a rip blade for cutting along the grain, and a crosscut blade for cutting across the grain.

b. Accurate Measurement and Marking: Before making any cuts, carefully measure and mark your workpiece to ensure accuracy and precision. Use a sharp pencil, marking knife, or gauge to create clear, visible lines to follow.

c. Securing Your Work: Always secure your workpiece firmly before making any cuts. Use clamps, vises, or other workholding devices to prevent your piece from shifting or vibrating during the cut.

d. Supporting Long Pieces: When cutting longer pieces of wood, provide adequate support to prevent sagging or binding. Use sawhorses, roller stands, or a helper to support the piece as you cut.

e. Proper Body Position: Maintain a stable, balanced stance when cutting, with your feet shoulder-width apart and your weight evenly distributed. Keep your hands and fingers away from the blade, and avoid reaching or overextending.

4. Shaping Techniques
In addition to cutting, there are several techniques used for shaping wood to create curved, rounded, or decorative elements. These include:

a. Planing: Using a hand plane or power planer to remove small amounts of wood and create a smooth, flat surface. Planing is often used for finishing or fitting pieces together.

b. Routing: Using a hand-held or table-mounted router to create grooves, dadoes, or decorative profiles in wood. Routers are versatile tools that can be used with a variety of bits and templates to create complex shapes and designs.

c. Sanding: Using abrasive paper or discs to smooth and shape wood surfaces. Sanding is often used for finishing or preparing wood for staining or painting.

d. Carving: Using hand chisels, gouges, or power carvers to create intricate designs, patterns, or sculptural elements in wood. Carving requires a high level of skill and artistry, but can add unique, personalized details to your projects.

5. Safety Considerations
Whenever cutting or shaping wood, it's essential to prioritize safety to prevent accidents or injuries. Here are some key safety considerations to keep in mind:

a. Wear Proper Safety Gear: Always wear eye and ear protection when using power tools, as well as a dust mask or respirator when sanding or creating significant amounts of sawdust. Consider wearing gloves or push sticks to protect your hands when working with sharp blades.

b. Inspect Your Tools: Before using any cutting or shaping tool, inspect it carefully for damage, wear, or malfunction. Ensure that blades are sharp, guards are in place, and all parts are securely attached and functioning properly.

c. Avoid Distractions: When operating cutting or shaping tools, stay focused and avoid distractions such as phone calls, conversations, or background noise. Maintain a clear, organized workspace to prevent tripping or accidental contact with tools.

d. Follow Manufacturer's Instructions: Always read and follow the manufacturer's instructions and safety guidelines for each tool you use. Use the tool only for its intended purpose, and avoid modifying or altering the tool in any way.

e. Keep Tools Clean and Maintained: Regularly clean and maintain your cutting and shaping tools to ensure optimal performance and safety. Sharpen blades, lubricate moving parts, and store tools properly to prevent damage or deterioration.

By mastering these cutting and shaping techniques and prioritizing safety in your woodworking practice, you can create precise, beautiful, and functional pieces that showcase your skill and craftsmanship. Whether you're using hand tools or power tools, the ability to cut and shape wood accurately and efficiently is a foundational skill that will serve you well in all your woodworking projects.

Sanding and Finishing

Sanding and finishing are the final steps in the woodworking process, and they play a crucial role in achieving a beautiful, durable, and professional-looking result. Sanding smooths and refines the wood surface, removing imperfections and preparing it for finishing, while finishing protects the wood from moisture, wear, and damage, and enhances its natural beauty and character. In this section, we'll explore the various techniques and materials used for sanding and finishing wood.

1. Sanding

Sanding is the process of using abrasive materials to smooth and refine the surface of the wood. There are several types of sanding materials and tools available, each with its own specific use and technique.

a. Sandpaper: The most common sanding material, sandpaper consists of abrasive particles bonded to a backing material, such as paper or cloth. Sandpaper is available in various grits, or levels of coarseness, ranging from very coarse (40-60 grit) for removing material quickly, to very fine (400-600 grit) for achieving a smooth, polished surface.

b. Sanding Blocks: Sanding blocks are flat, rectangular tools used to hold sandpaper and provide a firm, even surface for sanding. They can be made of wood, rubber, or foam, and are available in various sizes and shapes for different applications.

c. Power Sanders: Power sanders are electric tools that use a rotating or oscillating motion to sand wood surfaces quickly and efficiently. There are several types of power sanders, including belt sanders, orbital sanders, and detail sanders, each designed for specific tasks and materials.

d. Sanding Technique: When sanding, it's important to work with the grain of the wood, starting with a coarser grit and progressively moving to finer grits until the desired smoothness is achieved. Use light, even pressure, and avoid oversanding, which can create dips or unevenness in the surface.

2. Preparing for Finishing

Before applying any finish to your woodworking project, it's important to properly prepare the surface to ensure the best possible results. This involves several key steps:

a. Cleaning: Remove any dust, debris, or residue from the wood surface using a tack cloth, compressed air, or a vacuum with a brush attachment. Ensure that the surface is clean and dry before proceeding.

b. Grain Raising: Some woods, particularly those with open or porous grains, may require grain raising before finishing. This involves lightly dampening the surface with water, allowing it to dry, and then sanding it smooth. This process helps to raise and remove any loose fibers, creating a smoother, more receptive surface for the finish.

c. Filling: If your project has any cracks, knots, or imperfections that need to be filled, use a wood filler or epoxy to fill them in, then sand the area smooth once the filler has dried. Choose a filler that matches the color and grain of your wood for the best results.

d. Staining (optional): If you want to change the color of your wood or enhance its natural grain, you may choose to apply a stain before finishing. There are several types of stains available, including oil-based, water-based, and gel stains, each with its own application method and characteristics.

3. Types of Finishes

There are many different types of finishes available for woodworking projects, each with its own unique properties, appearance, and application method. Some of the most common types of finishes include:

a. Oil: Oil finishes, such as linseed oil or tung oil, penetrate the wood surface and provide a natural, low-sheen finish that enhances the wood's grain and character. They are easy to apply and maintain but may require multiple coats and regular reapplication.

b. Varnish: Varnish is a clear, hard, and durable finish that provides excellent protection against moisture, wear, and damage. It is available in various sheens, from matte to glossy, and can be brushed, sprayed, or wiped on.

c. Lacquer: Lacquer is a fast-drying, hard, and durable finish that provides a high-gloss, smooth surface. It is typically applied using a spray gun and requires multiple thin coats for the best results.

d. Shellac: Shellac is a natural, non-toxic finish made from the secretions of the lac bug. It dries quickly, provides a warm, amber tone, and is often used as a sealer or primer before applying other finishes.

e. Wax: Wax finishes, such as beeswax or carnauba wax, provide a soft, natural sheen and protection to the wood surface. They are easy to apply and maintain but may require regular reapplication.

4. Finishing Techniques

The specific finishing technique you use will depend on the type of finish you have chosen and the desired result. However, there are some general guidelines to keep in mind:

a. Read the Instructions: Before applying any finish, carefully read and follow the manufacturer's instructions for application, drying time, and safety precautions.

b. Work in a Clean, Dust-Free Environment: Dust and debris can ruin a finish, so make sure to work in a clean, well-ventilated space and use a tack cloth or compressed air to remove any particles before and between coats.

c. Use Quality Tools: Invest in high-quality brushes, rags, or sprayers for applying your finish, as cheap or low-quality tools can leave streaks, bubbles, or other imperfections in the surface.

d. Apply Thin, Even Coats: When applying a finish, use thin, even coats and avoid overloading your brush or applicator. Multiple thin coats will provide better coverage and durability than a single thick coat.

e. Sand Between Coats: For the smoothest, most professional-looking results, lightly sand the surface with fine-grit sandpaper (220-400 grit) between coats of finish. This helps to remove any dust nibs, brush marks, or other imperfections and creates a smooth surface for the next coat to adhere to.

5. Maintenance and Repair

Even with the most careful sanding and finishing, wood surfaces can still be susceptible to damage, wear, and aging over time. To keep your woodworking projects looking their best, it's important to properly maintain and repair them as needed.

a. Regular Cleaning: Dust and clean your wood surfaces regularly using a soft, dry cloth or a vacuum with a brush attachment. Avoid using harsh chemicals or abrasive cleaners, which can damage the finish or the wood itself.

b. Refreshing the Finish: Over time, some finishes may dull or lose their luster. To refresh the finish, you can lightly sand the surface with fine-grit sandpaper and apply a new coat of the same finish, or use a compatible polish or wax to restore the shine.

c. Repairing Damage: If your wood surface becomes scratched, dented, or otherwise damaged, there are several techniques for repairing it, depending on the extent of the damage. Minor scratches can often be buffed out with fine steel wool or a compatible wax or polish, while deeper scratches or dents may require filling with a wood filler or epoxy, then sanding and refinishing the area.

d. Protecting from Environmental Factors: To prevent damage from moisture, sunlight, or temperature fluctuations, use coasters, placemats, or runners to protect wood surfaces from spills or hot dishes, and avoid placing wood furniture in direct sunlight or near heat sources. Consider using a humidifier or dehumidifier to maintain a consistent humidity level in your home, which can help prevent cracking, warping, or other moisture-related damage.

By mastering these sanding and finishing techniques and properly maintaining your woodworking projects, you can achieve beautiful, long-lasting results that showcase your skill and craftsmanship. Whether you're working on a simple DIY project or a complex piece of furniture, the ability to sand and finish wood effectively is a valuable skill that will serve you well in all your woodworking endeavors.

Chapter 3
Building Custom Shelves
Designing Functional and Stylish Shelves

Custom shelves are a practical and stylish addition to any home, providing both storage and display space for books, decorative items, and other belongings. Building your own shelves allows you to create a design that perfectly fits your space, style, and needs, while also showcasing your woodworking skills and creativity. In this section, we'll explore the process of designing and building functional and stylish custom shelves.

Designing Functional and Stylish Shelves

1. Assess Your Space and Needs
Before designing your custom shelves, it's important to carefully assess the space where they will be installed and consider your specific storage and display needs.

a. Measure the Area: Use a tape measure to accurately measure the width, height, and depth of the space where you plan to install your shelves. Take note of any obstacles or features that may impact your design, such as windows, doors, or electrical outlets.

b. Consider Your Storage Needs: Think about what you plan to store or display on your shelves, and how much space you will need for each item. Consider the size, weight, and quantity of your belongings, as well as how often you will need to access them.

c. Determine the Number of Shelves: Based on your storage needs and the available space, determine the number of shelves you will need and the spacing between them. A general rule of thumb is to space shelves about 12-15 inches apart for books, and 18-24 inches apart for larger items.

2. Choose a Style and Material

Once you have assessed your space and needs, you can begin to explore different styles and materials for your custom shelves.

a. Shelf Styles: There are many different styles of shelves to choose from, ranging from simple, minimalist designs to more elaborate, decorative styles. Some popular shelf styles include:

- Floating Shelves: Shelves that appear to "float" on the wall, with no visible brackets or supports.
- Bracketed Shelves: Shelves that are supported by visible brackets or braces, which can be decorative or industrial in style.
- Built-In Shelves: Shelves that are permanently installed into the wall or surrounding cabinetry, creating a seamless, integrated look.
- Adjustable Shelves: Shelves that can be easily moved or reconfigured using a system of pins, clips, or tracks.

b. Material Options: The material you choose for your shelves will impact their durability, appearance, and cost. Some popular material options for custom shelves include:

- Wood: A classic and versatile option, wood shelves can be made from a variety of species, such as pine, oak, or walnut, and can be stained or painted to match your décor.
- Medium-Density Fiberboard (MDF): A cost-effective and stable alternative to solid wood, MDF is made from wood fibers and resin and can be painted or laminated for a smooth, durable finish.
- Plywood: A strong and lightweight option, plywood is made from thin layers of wood veneer and can be stained or painted to achieve various looks.
- Metal: Metal shelves, such as those made from steel or aluminum, offer a modern, industrial look and are highly durable and easy to clean.

3. Create a Design Plan

With your style and material choices in mind, you can now create a detailed design plan for your custom shelves. This plan should include:

a. Dimensions: The exact measurements of each shelf, including width, depth, and thickness, as well as the overall dimensions of the shelving unit.

b. Support Structure: The type and placement of brackets, braces, or other supports that will hold the shelves in place. Consider the weight and size of the items you plan to store, and choose a support system that is strong and secure.

c. Mounting Method: The method you will use to attach the shelves to the wall or surrounding structure. This may involve drilling into studs, using drywall anchors, or creating a custom mounting system.

d. Finishing Details: Any decorative details or finishing touches you want to include, such as molding, trim, or edge banding. Consider how these details will impact the overall look and function of your shelves.

4. Gather Materials and Tools

With your design plan in hand, you can now gather the necessary materials and tools to build your custom shelves. This may include:

a. Lumber or Sheet Goods: The wood or MDF needed to create the shelves and support structure, cut to the appropriate dimensions.

b. Hardware: Any brackets, braces, screws, anchors, or other hardware needed to assemble and mount the shelves.

c. Finishing Supplies: Sandpaper, stain, paint, or other finishing materials needed to achieve your desired look.

d. Tools: The necessary tools for cutting, drilling, sanding, and assembling your shelves, such as a saw, drill, level, and clamps.

5. Cut and Assemble the Shelves

With your materials and tools gathered, you can now begin the process of cutting and assembling your custom shelves.

a. Cut the Shelf Pieces: Using your design plan as a guide, carefully measure and cut the lumber or sheet goods to the appropriate dimensions for each shelf. Use a saw or power tool appropriate for your material, such as a table saw for wood or a circular saw for MDF.

b. Sand and Finish the Pieces: Before assembly, sand each shelf piece to remove any rough edges or splinters. If desired, apply stain, paint, or other finishing materials at this stage, following the manufacturer's instructions for application and drying time.

c. Assemble the Shelves: Using your chosen support structure and hardware, assemble the shelves according to your design plan. Take care to ensure that each shelf is level, straight, and securely attached to the supports.

d. Mount the Shelves: Following your mounting plan, carefully install the assembled shelves onto the wall or surrounding structure. Use a level to ensure that the shelves are straight and even, and take care to securely fasten the shelves using the appropriate hardware and techniques.

6. Add Finishing Touches

With your custom shelves installed, you can now add any finishing touches or decorative elements to complete the look.

a. Add Molding or Trim: If desired, add molding or trim to the edges of the shelves or surrounding structure to create a polished, finished look. Miter the corners for a seamless appearance, and attach the trim using finishing nails or adhesive.

b. Install Lighting: Consider adding lighting to your shelves to highlight your display items and create a warm, inviting atmosphere. Options may include LED strip lights, puck lights, or battery-operated lights that can be easily installed and adjusted.

c. Style and Decorate: Finally, style and decorate your new custom shelves with your favorite books, art, plants, or other display items. Arrange the items in a way that is both functional and visually appealing, and adjust them over time as your needs and preferences change.

By following these steps and using your creativity and woodworking skills, you can design and build custom shelves that are both functional and stylish, and that perfectly fit your space and needs. Whether you're creating a simple bookshelf or a complex built-in unit, the process of designing and building custom shelves is a rewarding and satisfying project that will add value and character to your home for years to come.

Wall-Mounted Shelf Construction

Wall-mounted shelves are a popular and versatile option for adding storage and display space to any room in your home. By attaching the shelves directly to the wall, you can create a clean, minimalist look that maximizes floor space and allows for easy customization and rearrangement. In this section, we'll explore the process of constructing and installing wall-mounted shelves, including the tools and materials needed, the basic steps involved, and some tips and considerations for ensuring a secure and successful installation.

1. Tools and Materials

Before beginning your wall-mounted shelf project, it's important to gather all the necessary tools and materials. This may include:

a. Lumber or Sheet Goods: The wood or MDF needed to create the shelves themselves, cut to the appropriate dimensions.

b. Mounting Hardware: The screws, anchors, or other hardware needed to attach the shelves to the wall. The type of hardware will depend on the weight and size of the shelves, as well as the type of wall material (e.g., drywall, plaster, brick).

c. Drill and Bits: A power drill and appropriate drill bits for creating pilot holes and driving screws.

d. Level: A carpenter's level or laser level for ensuring that the shelves are straight and even.

e. Stud Finder: A tool for locating the studs in your wall, which will provide the most secure mounting points for your shelves.

f. Saw: A handsaw, circular saw, or table saw for cutting the shelf material to size.

g. Sandpaper: Coarse and fine-grit sandpaper for smoothing the edges and surfaces of the shelves.

h. Finishing Supplies: Stain, paint, or other finishing materials for protecting and enhancing the appearance of the shelves.

2. Preparing the Wall
Before installing your wall-mounted shelves, it's important to properly prepare the wall to ensure a secure and stable installation.

a. Locate the Studs: Use a stud finder to locate the studs in your wall, which are typically spaced 16 or 24 inches apart. Mark the location of each stud with a pencil or painter's tape.

b. Determine the Shelf Placement: Decide on the desired height and placement of your shelves, taking into account the size and spacing of the items you plan to store or display. Use a level to mark a straight, horizontal line at the desired height for each shelf.

c. Drill Pilot Holes: At each stud location along the marked line, drill a pilot hole for your mounting screws. The size of the pilot hole will depend on the size of your screws and the type of wall material.

3. Cutting and Finishing the Shelves
With the wall prepared, you can now cut and finish the shelf material to the appropriate size and style.

a. Measure and Cut the Shelves: Measure the distance between the pilot holes on your wall, and cut your shelf material to the appropriate length using a saw. If desired, you can also cut the shelves to a specific depth or width, depending on your storage needs and aesthetic preferences.

b. Sand and Finish the Shelves: Use sandpaper to smooth any rough edges or surfaces on the shelves, starting with a coarse grit and progressing to a finer grit for a smooth finish. If desired, apply stain, paint, or other finishing materials to the shelves, following the manufacturer's instructions for application and drying time.

4. Installing the Shelves
With the shelves cut and finished, you can now install them on the wall using your chosen mounting hardware.

a. Attach Mounting Hardware: If using brackets or other visible hardware, attach them to the shelves using screws or adhesive, following the manufacturer's instructions. If using hidden hardware, such as keyhole hangers or French cleats, attach them to the back of the shelves at the appropriate locations.

b. Mount the Shelves: Align the shelves with the pilot holes on the wall, and use a drill or screwdriver to secure the mounting screws into the studs. Use a level to ensure that each shelf is straight and even as you attach it to the wall.

c. Test the Strength: After installing each shelf, test its strength and stability by gently pushing down on it and checking for any movement or·wobbling. If necessary, tighten the screws or add additional support to ensure a secure installation.

5. Tips and Considerations
To ensure a successful and long-lasting wall-mounted shelf installation, consider the following tips and considerations:

a. Use Appropriate Hardware: Choose mounting hardware that is appropriate for the weight and size of your shelves, as well as the type of wall material. When in doubt, err on the side of stronger, more robust hardware to ensure a secure installation.

b. Reinforce Heavy Shelves: For particularly heavy or deep shelves, consider using additional support, such as metal brackets or a plywood backing, to distribute the weight and prevent sagging or bowing over time.

c. Consider Adjustable Shelving: If your storage needs may change over time, consider using adjustable shelf hardware, such as standards and brackets, which allow you to easily move or reconfigure the shelves as needed.

d. Plan for Electrical and Plumbing: Before installing shelves on a wall, use a stud finder or other tool to locate any electrical wires, plumbing pipes, or other obstacles that may be hidden behind the wall. Avoid drilling or mounting shelves in these areas to prevent damage or safety hazards.

e. Add Decorative Touches: To enhance the appearance of your wall-mounted shelves, consider adding decorative touches, such as molding, trim, or lighting, to create a polished, personalized look.

By following these steps and considering these tips, you can construct and install wall-mounted shelves that are both functional and attractive, and that provide a customized storage and display solution for your home. Whether you're creating a simple shelf for books and decor, or a complex system of adjustable shelving for a home office or workshop, the process of constructing wall-mounted shelves is a rewarding and practical project that can add value and versatility to any space.

Freestanding Bookshelf Project

A freestanding bookshelf is a versatile and practical addition to any home, providing ample storage space for books, magazines, and other items while also serving as an attractive piece of furniture. Building your own freestanding bookshelf allows you to customize the size, style, and features to perfectly suit your space and needs, while also showcasing your woodworking skills and creativity. In this section, we'll explore the process of designing, constructing, and finishing a freestanding bookshelf project, including the tools and materials needed, the basic steps involved, and some tips and variations for creating a unique and functional piece.

1. Design Considerations

Before beginning your freestanding bookshelf project, it's important to carefully consider your design goals and constraints, including:

a. Size and Proportions: Determine the desired height, width, and depth of your bookshelf based on the available space in your room and the size of the items you plan to store. Consider the proportions of the shelves in relation to the overall unit, as well as the spacing between the shelves for optimal storage and accessibility.

b. Style and Aesthetics: Choose a style for your bookshelf that complements the existing decor and architecture of your room. Consider factors such as the type of wood, the finish or color, and any decorative details or embellishments that will enhance the overall look of the piece.

c. Install Adjustable Shelves: If using adjustable shelf pins, insert the pins into the pre-drilled holes and place the shelves on top, making sure that they are level and stable.

c. Structural Integrity: Ensure that your design includes adequate structural support for the weight and size of the items you plan to store. Consider the thickness and spacing of the shelves, the type of joinery used for the frame, and any additional bracing or reinforcement that may be needed for stability.

d. Adjustability and Customization: Decide whether you want your bookshelf to have fixed or adjustable shelves, and consider any additional features or customizations that may enhance its functionality, such as drawers, doors, or built-in lighting.

2. Tools and Materials
To build a freestanding bookshelf, you will need the following tools and materials:

a. Lumber: Choose a suitable wood species for your project, such as pine, oak, or walnut, and purchase the necessary boards and plywood in the appropriate dimensions.

b. Hardware: Gather any hardware needed for the project, such as screws, nails, shelf pins, and brackets.

c. Saws: You will need a table saw, miter saw, or circular saw to make precise cuts for the frame and shelves.

d. Drill and Bits: A power drill and various drill bits will be needed for creating pilot holes and driving screws.

e. Sander: A random orbital sander or belt sander will be used to smooth the surfaces of the wood before finishing.

f. Clamps: Various clamps, such as bar clamps or pipe clamps, will be needed to hold the pieces together during assembly.

g. Measuring and Marking Tools: You will need a tape measure, carpenter's square, and pencil for accurately measuring and marking the wood.

h. Safety Equipment: Always wear appropriate safety gear, such as eye protection, ear protection, and a dust mask, when working with power tools and wood.

3. Cutting and Preparing the Pieces
With your design and materials in hand, you can now begin cutting and preparing the pieces for your freestanding bookshelf.

a. Cut the Frame Pieces: Using your saws and measuring tools, cut the top, bottom, and side pieces for the bookshelf frame to the appropriate dimensions, taking care to ensure that the cuts are straight and accurate.

b. Cut the Shelves: Measure and cut the shelves to the desired width and depth, making sure to account for any dadoes or rabbets that will be used to secure the shelves to the frame.

c. Drill Shelf Pin Holes (Optional): If you plan to use adjustable shelf pins, drill evenly spaced holes along the inside of the side pieces to accommodate the pins.

d. Sand the Pieces: Use your sander to smooth all surfaces and edges of the frame and shelf pieces, progressing from coarse to fine grit sandpaper for a smooth, even finish.

4. Assembling the Bookshelf
With the pieces cut and prepared, you can now assemble the freestanding bookshelf using your chosen joinery method.

a. Attach the Frame Pieces: Using screws, nails, or wood glue, attach the top, bottom, and side pieces of the frame together, making sure that the corners are square and the pieces are flush.

b. Install Fixed Shelves: If your design includes fixed shelves, attach them to the frame using dadoes, rabbets, or cleats, ensuring that they are level and securely fastened.

d. Add Backing (Optional): If desired, attach a thin plywood backing to the rear of the bookshelf frame using nails or screws to provide additional stability and a finished look.

5. Finishing and Customization
With the bookshelf assembled, you can now add any finishing touches or customizations to enhance its appearance and functionality.

a. Sand and Finish: Give the entire bookshelf a final sanding with fine-grit sandpaper, then apply your chosen finish, such as stain, paint, or clear coat, following the manufacturer's instructions for application and drying time.

b. Add Decorative Details: If desired, add any decorative details or embellishments to the bookshelf, such as molding, trim, or inlays, to enhance its visual appeal.

c. Install Lighting (Optional): Consider installing built-in lighting, such as LED strips or puck lights, to illuminate the shelves and create a warm, inviting ambiance.

d. Customize with Doors or Drawers (Optional): For added functionality and style, consider incorporating doors or drawers into your bookshelf design, using appropriate hardware and joinery techniques.

By following these steps and considering your specific design goals and preferences, you can create a freestanding bookshelf that is both functional and beautiful, and that reflects your unique style and craftsmanship. Whether you're building a simple, minimalist shelf or an elaborate, multi-functional unit, the process of designing and constructing a freestanding bookshelf is a rewarding and practical project that can add value and character to any room in your home.

Decorative Floating Shelves

Floating shelves have become an increasingly popular design element in modern homes, offering a sleek, minimalist look while providing functional storage and display space. Unlike traditional shelves that are visibly supported by brackets or frames, floating shelves appear to "float" on the wall, creating an illusion of weightlessness and a clean, uncluttered aesthetic. In this section, we'll explore the process of designing, constructing, and installing decorative floating shelves, including the tools and materials needed, the basic steps involved, and some tips and variations for creating a stylish and functional addition to your home decor.

1. Design Considerations

When designing your decorative floating shelves, consider the following factors to ensure a successful and visually appealing result:

a. Size and Placement: Determine the desired length, width, and thickness of your shelves based on the available wall space and the items you plan to display. Consider the placement of the shelves in relation to other wall features, such as windows, doors, or artwork, to create a balanced and harmonious composition.

b. Material and Finish: Choose a material and finish for your shelves that complements the existing style and color palette of your room. Popular options include solid wood, laminated wood, or medium-density fiberboard (MDF) with a painted, stained, or veneered finish.

c. Weight Capacity: Ensure that your floating shelf design can support the weight of the items you plan to display, taking into account the thickness of the shelf material and the type of mounting hardware used.

d. Style and Aesthetics: Consider the overall style and visual impact of your floating shelves, including the shape of the shelves (rectangular, square, or curved), the edge profile (straight, rounded, or beveled), and any decorative details or accents (such as recessed lighting or integrated cable management).

2. Tools and Materials

To construct and install decorative floating shelves, you will need the following tools and materials:

a. Shelf Material: Choose a suitable material for your shelves, such as solid wood, plywood, or MDF, in the desired thickness and dimensions.

b. Mounting Hardware: Select appropriate hardware for securely attaching the shelves to the wall, such as hidden bracket systems, metal cleats, or toggle bolts, depending on the weight capacity and wall type.

c. Power Tools: You will need a drill, circular saw, and jigsaw for cutting and shaping the shelf material, as well as a stud finder for locating wall studs.

d. Sanding and Finishing Supplies: Gather sandpaper, wood filler, primer, paint or stain, and clear coat for preparing and finishing the shelf surfaces.

e. Measuring and Marking Tools: You will need a tape measure, level, pencil, and carpenter's square for accurately measuring and marking the shelf positions and dimensions.

f. Safety Equipment: Always wear appropriate safety gear, such as eye protection, ear protection, and a dust mask, when working with power tools and wood.

3. Constructing the Shelves

With your design and materials in hand, follow these steps to construct your decorative floating shelves:

a. Cut the Shelf Material: Using your circular saw or jigsaw, cut the shelf material to the desired dimensions, taking care to ensure straight and accurate cuts.

b. Sand and Finish the Shelves: Sand the shelf surfaces and edges with progressively finer grits of sandpaper until smooth, then apply wood filler to any cracks or imperfections. Once dry, sand the filler smooth and apply primer, paint, or stain, and clear coat according to the manufacturer's instructions.

c. Attach Mounting Hardware: Depending on your chosen mounting system, attach the appropriate hardware to the back or underside of the shelves, such as hidden brackets, metal cleats, or keyhole hangers, ensuring a secure and level fit.

4. Installing the Shelves

With the shelves constructed and finished, follow these steps to install them on your wall:

a. Mark the Shelf Positions: Using a level and pencil, mark the desired positions of the shelves on the wall, ensuring that they are straight and evenly spaced.

b. Locate Wall Studs: Use a stud finder to locate the wall studs closest to your marked shelf positions, as attaching the shelves directly to studs will provide the most secure and stable installation.

c. Attach Wall Mounting Hardware: Depending on your chosen mounting system, attach the corresponding hardware to the wall at the marked positions, such as hidden bracket receivers, metal cleats, or toggle bolt anchors, ensuring that they are level and securely fastened.

d. Hang the Shelves: Carefully align the shelves with the wall mounting hardware and secure them in place, checking for level and stability.

5. Styling and Customization
Once your decorative floating shelves are installed, you can enhance their visual impact and functionality with these styling and customization tips:

a. Create Visual Balance: When styling your shelves, consider the balance and composition of the displayed items, using a mix of larger and smaller objects, and varying the heights and textures for visual interest.

b. Incorporate Lighting: Add integrated lighting to your floating shelves, such as recessed LED strips or puck lights, to highlight the displayed items and create a warm, inviting ambiance.

c. Add Decorative Accents: Customize your shelves with decorative accents, such as sconces, plants, or artwork, to complement the displayed items and enhance the overall aesthetic of the room.

d. Use Color and Texture: Experiment with different colors, finishes, and textures for your floating shelves, such as natural wood grain, metallic accents, or bold painted hues, to create a unique and personalized look.

By following these steps and considering your specific design goals and preferences, you can create stunning decorative floating shelves that add both style and function to your home decor. Whether you're displaying cherished photographs, collectibles, or everyday objects, floating shelves offer a versatile and contemporary solution for showcasing your personal style and maximizing your wall space. With a little creativity and attention to detail, your custom floating shelves can become a beautiful and practical focal point in any room of your home.

Chapter 4
Crafting Interior Trim
Baseboards and Crown Molding Installation

Interior trim, such as baseboards and crown molding, plays a crucial role in enhancing the aesthetics and character of a room. These decorative elements provide a finished look, conceal gaps and imperfections, and create a seamless transition between walls, floors, and ceilings. Installing baseboards and crown molding requires precision, patience, and attention to detail, but the end result is a polished and sophisticated look that adds value and charm to any interior space. In this section, we'll explore the process of crafting interior trim, focusing on the installation of baseboards and crown molding, including the tools and materials needed, the basic steps involved, and some tips and techniques for achieving professional-looking results.

1. Tools and Materials
   Before beginning your interior trim project, gather the following essential tools and materials:

   a. Trim Material: Select the appropriate trim material for your project, such as wood, MDF, or PVC, in the desired style, width, and thickness.

   b. Miter Saw: A miter saw is essential for making precise angled cuts in the trim material, such as 45-degree angles for corner joints.

   c. Nail Gun or Hammer: Use a finish nail gun or hammer to attach the trim to the walls, ensuring a secure and flush fit.

d. Measuring and Marking Tools: You'll need a tape measure, pencil, and combination square for accurately measuring and marking the trim pieces.

e. Coping Saw: A coping saw is used for making intricate cuts in the trim, such as coped joints for inside corners.

f. Sandpaper and Putty: Use sandpaper to smooth any rough edges or imperfections in the trim, and wood putty to fill nail holes and gaps.

g. Paint or Stain: Choose a paint or stain color that complements your interior design, and gather the necessary brushes, rollers, and drop cloths.

h. Safety Equipment: Always wear appropriate safety gear, such as eye protection and a dust mask, when working with power tools and wood.

2. Preparing the Room

Before installing the trim, take the time to properly prepare the room for a smooth and efficient installation process:

a. Clear the Area: Remove any furniture, rugs, or decor from the room, and cover the floors with drop cloths to protect them from dust and debris.

b. Clean and Repair Walls: Fill any cracks, holes, or imperfections in the walls with joint compound, and sand smooth once dry. Wipe down the walls to remove dust and ensure a clean surface for the trim installation.

c. Remove Old Trim: If replacing existing trim, carefully remove the old pieces using a pry bar or putty knife, taking care not to damage the walls or floors.

d. Plan the Layout: Measure the room and sketch a layout of the trim design, noting the locations of inside and outside corners, doors, and windows, and calculating the necessary trim lengths.

3. Installing Baseboards
Follow these steps to successfully install baseboards in your room:

a. Measure and Cut: Measure the length of each wall and cut the baseboard pieces to size using a miter saw, adding a 45-degree angle at the ends for corner joints.

b. Dry Fit: Before attaching the baseboards, dry fit the pieces along the walls to ensure a proper fit and make any necessary adjustments.

c. Attach the Trim: Using a finish nail gun or hammer, attach the baseboards to the walls, starting at one corner and working your way around the room. Ensure that the trim is level and flush against the wall and floor.

d. Cope Inside Corners: For a seamless look at inside corners, use a coping saw to cut a matching profile on the end of one baseboard piece, allowing it to fit snugly against the adjoining piece.

e. Fill and Sand: Once the baseboards are installed, fill any nail holes or gaps with wood putty, let dry, and sand smooth. Wipe away any dust with a tack cloth.

4. Installing Crown Molding
Crown molding adds an elegant and sophisticated touch to any room. Follow these steps for a successful installation:

a. Measure and Cut: Measure the length of each wall and cut the crown molding pieces to size using a miter saw, cutting a 45-degree angle at the ends for corner joints. For inside corners, cut a 45-degree angle in the opposite direction.

b. Mark the Wall: Using a pencil and level, mark a line along the wall where the top of the crown molding will sit, ensuring that it is level and at the desired height.

c. Attach the Trim: Using a finish nail gun or hammer, attach the crown molding to the wall, starting at one corner and working your way around the room. Ensure that the trim is level and flush against the wall and ceiling.

d. Cope Inside Corners: Similar to baseboards, use a coping saw to cut a matching profile on the end of one crown molding piece for a seamless fit at inside corners.

e. Fill and Sand: Once the crown molding is installed, fill any nail holes or gaps with wood putty, let dry, and sand smooth. Wipe away any dust with a tack cloth.

5. Finishing and Painting
After installing the baseboards and crown molding, add the finishing touches to complete the look:

a. Sand and Prime: Lightly sand the trim with fine-grit sandpaper to ensure a smooth surface, then apply a coat of primer to help the paint adhere better and last longer.

b. Paint or Stain: Once the primer is dry, apply your chosen paint or stain color to the trim, using a brush or roller for even coverage. Apply additional coats as needed, allowing each coat to dry completely before applying the next.

c. Caulk Gaps: Use a paintable caulk to fill any remaining gaps between the trim and the walls or ceiling, creating a seamless and finished look. Smooth the caulk with a wet finger or caulk tool, and touch up with paint as needed.

By following these steps and paying attention to the details, you can successfully craft beautiful and professional-looking interior trim that enhances the character and value of your home. Whether you're installing classic wooden baseboards or elegant crown molding, the process of crafting interior trim is a rewarding and satisfying project that allows you to showcase your woodworking skills and create a polished and inviting living space. With the right tools, materials, and techniques, you can achieve stunning results that you'll be proud to showcase for years to come.

Door and Window Casing Techniques

Door and window casings are essential elements of interior trim that serve both functional and decorative purposes. These trim pieces surround the openings of doors and windows, concealing the gaps between the frames and the wall, while also adding visual interest and character to the room. Installing door and window casings requires precision, skill, and an understanding of various techniques to achieve a professional and polished look. In this section, we'll explore the different techniques used for installing door and window casings, including the tools and materials needed, the basic steps involved, and some tips and variations for creating a custom and stylish finish.

1. Tools and Materials

To successfully install door and window casings, you'll need the following tools and materials:

a. Casing Material: Choose the appropriate casing material for your project, such as wood, MDF, or PVC, in the desired style, width, and thickness.

b. Miter Saw: A miter saw is essential for making precise angled cuts in the casing material, such as 45-degree angles for corner joints.

c. Nail Gun or Hammer: Use a finish nail gun or hammer to attach the casing to the door or window frame and the wall.

d. Measuring and Marking Tools: You'll need a tape measure, pencil, and combination square for accurately measuring and marking the casing pieces.

f. Sandpaper and Putty: Use sandpaper to smooth any rough edges or imperfections in the casing, and wood putty to fill nail holes and gaps.

g. Paint or Stain: Choose a paint or stain color that complements your interior design, and gather the necessary brushes, rollers, and drop cloths.

2. Measuring and Cutting

Accurate measuring and cutting are crucial for achieving a precise and professional-looking casing installation. Follow these tips for success:

a. Measure the Opening: Measure the height and width of the door or window opening, including the frame, and add the desired casing width to each measurement to determine the overall casing dimensions.

b. Cut the Casing: Using a miter saw, cut the casing pieces to the appropriate lengths, with 45-degree angles at the ends for corner joints. For a more decorative look, consider adding a profile or beveled edge to the casing using a router or specialized saw blade.

c. Label the Pieces: As you cut each casing piece, label it according to its location (e.g., "top," "left side," "right side") to ensure a smooth and organized installation process.

3. Installation Techniques

There are several techniques for installing door and window casings, each with its own advantages and considerations:

a. Butted Joints: The simplest installation technique involves cutting the casing pieces to fit tightly against each other at the corners, creating a clean and minimalist look. This method works best with thinner, less ornate casing styles.

b. Mitered Joints: For a more traditional and polished look, cut the casing pieces at 45-degree angles and join them at the corners to create a mitered joint. This technique requires precise cuts and a bit more skill but results in a seamless and attractive finish.

c. Coped Joints: Coped joints involve using a coping saw to cut a profile on the end of one casing piece that fits snugly against the face of the adjoining piece. This technique is ideal for inside corners and can accommodate slight irregularities in the wall or frame.

d. Layered Casings: For a more elaborate and custom look, consider layering multiple casing pieces of different widths and profiles to create a dimensional and sculptural effect. This technique allows for greater creativity and can be tailored to match specific architectural styles.

4. Attaching the Casing
Once your casing pieces are cut and ready, follow these steps to attach them to the door or window frame and wall:

a. Start with the Top Piece: Begin by attaching the top casing piece, ensuring that it is level and centered over the opening. Use a finish nail gun or hammer to secure the casing to the frame and wall, driving the nails at an angle for a stronger hold.

e. Coping Saw: A coping saw is used for making intricate cuts in the casing, such as coped joints for inside corners.

b. Install the Side Pieces: Next, attach the side casing pieces, making sure they are plumb (vertically straight) and tightly fitted against the top piece. Use a combination square to check for square corners and adjust as needed.

c. Secure the Bottom Piece: Finally, attach the bottom casing piece, ensuring that it is level and tightly fitted against the side pieces. If the floor is uneven, you may need to scribe the bottom of the casing to match the contour of the floor for a seamless fit.

d. Fill and Sand: Once the casing is installed, fill any nail holes or gaps with wood putty, let dry, and sand smooth. Wipe away any dust with a tack cloth.

5. Finishing and Painting
After installing the door and window casings, add the finishing touches to complete the look:

a. Sand and Prime: Lightly sand the casing with fine-grit sandpaper to ensure a smooth surface, then apply a coat of primer to help the paint adhere better and last longer.

b. Paint or Stain: Once the primer is dry, apply your chosen paint or stain color to the casing, using a brush or roller for even coverage. Apply additional coats as needed, allowing each coat to dry completely before applying the next.

c. Caulk Gaps: Use a paintable caulk to fill any remaining gaps between the casing and the wall or frame, creating a seamless and finished look. Smooth the caulk with a wet finger or caulk tool, and touch up with paint as needed.

By mastering these door and window casing techniques and paying attention to the details, you can create a polished and professional-looking finish that enhances the beauty and character of your home. Whether you opt for a simple and minimalist casing style or a more elaborate and decorative design, the process of installing door and window casings is a rewarding and satisfying project that allows you to showcase your woodworking skills and elevate the overall look and feel of your interior space.

With the right tools, materials, and techniques, you can achieve stunning results that you'll be proud to showcase for years to come.

Wainscoting and Chair Rail Projects

Wainscoting and chair rails are classic architectural elements that add depth, character, and visual interest to interior walls. Wainscoting refers to decorative paneling that typically covers the lower portion of a wall, while a chair rail is a horizontal molding installed at chair height, originally designed to protect walls from damage caused by chairs. These elements can be used together or separately to create a variety of stylish and functional looks, from traditional and elegant to modern and minimalist. In this section, we'll explore the process of designing and installing wainscoting and chair rail projects, including the tools and materials needed, the basic steps involved, and some tips and variations for achieving a professional and polished result.

1. Design Considerations

Before beginning your wainscoting or chair rail project, consider the following design factors to ensure a successful and cohesive look:

a. Style and Pattern: Choose a wainscoting style and pattern that complements the existing architecture and decor of your room. Popular options include raised panels, beadboard, board and batten, and recessed panels.

b. Height and Proportion: Determine the desired height of your wainscoting or chair rail based on the room's dimensions, ceiling height, and overall proportions. A general rule of thumb is to install chair rails at one-third the height of the room, while wainscoting typically ranges from one-third to two-thirds of the wall height.

c. Material and Finish: Select a material and finish for your wainscoting or chair rail that suits your budget, durability needs, and aesthetic preferences. Options include solid wood, MDF, PVC, and pre-primed or painted panels.

d. Trim and Details: Consider adding decorative trim or details to your wainscoting or chair rail, such as base caps, corner blocks, or molded profiles, to enhance the visual interest and custom look of your project.

2. Tools and Materials

To successfully install wainscoting or chair rails, you'll need the following tools and materials:

a. Paneling or Molding Material: Choose the appropriate paneling or molding material for your project, such as solid wood, MDF, or PVC, in the desired style, width, and thickness.

b. Miter Saw or Circular Saw: Use a miter saw or circular saw to make precise cuts in the paneling or molding material, such as 45-degree angles for corner joints.

c. Nail Gun or Hammer: Use a finish nail gun or hammer to attach the paneling or molding to the wall, ensuring a secure and flush fit.

d. Measuring and Marking Tools: You'll need a tape measure, level, pencil, and combination square for accurately measuring and marking the paneling or molding pieces.

e. Stud Finder: Use a stud finder to locate and mark the wall studs, which will provide a secure anchoring point for the paneling or molding.

f. Sandpaper and Putty: Use sandpaper to smooth any rough edges or imperfections in the paneling or molding, and wood putty to fill nail holes and gaps.

g. Paint or Stain: Choose a paint or stain color that complements your interior design, and gather the necessary brushes, rollers, and drop cloths.

3. Installing Wainscoting
Follow these steps to successfully install wainscoting in your room:

a. Prepare the Wall: Remove any existing baseboards or trim, fill any cracks or holes with joint compound, and sand the wall smooth. Use a stud finder to locate and mark the wall studs.

b. Measure and Cut the Panels: Measure the height and width of the wall and cut the wainscoting panels to size using a miter saw or circular saw. If using a patterned design, like beadboard, consider the placement of the grooves for a symmetrical look.

c. Install the Panels: Starting at one corner of the room, attach the wainscoting panels to the wall using a nail gun or hammer, ensuring that the panels are level, plumb, and tightly fitted together. Use a level to check for straightness and make adjustments as needed.

d. Add Trim and Details: Once the panels are installed, add any desired trim or decorative details, such as base caps, chair rails, or corner blocks, using a nail gun or hammer and mitered cuts for corner joints.

e. Fill, Sand, and Paint: Fill any nail holes or gaps with wood putty, let dry, and sand smooth. Apply your chosen paint or stain color, using a brush or roller for even coverage, and allow to dry completely.

4. Installing Chair Rails

Follow these steps to successfully install chair rails in your room:

a. Measure and Mark: Measure the desired height of the chair rail from the floor and mark a level line around the room using a pencil and level. Use a stud finder to locate and mark the wall studs along the line.

b. Cut the Molding: Measure the length of each wall and cut the chair rail molding to size using a miter saw, with 45-degree angles at the ends for corner joints.

c. Install the Molding: Starting at one corner of the room, attach the chair rail molding to the wall using a nail gun or hammer, ensuring that the molding is level and tightly fitted at the corner joints. Use a level to check for straightness and make adjustments as needed.

d. Fill, Sand, and Paint: Fill any nail holes or gaps with wood putty, let dry, and sand smooth. Apply your chosen paint or stain color, using a brush or roller for even coverage, and allow to dry completely.

5. Customization and Variation

To create a unique and personalized look, consider these customization and variation ideas for your wainscoting or chair rail project:

a. Two-Tone Color Scheme: Paint the wainscoting or chair rail a different color than the upper portion of the wall for a bold and contrasting look.

b. Wallpaper Accent: Use wallpaper above the chair rail or within the wainscoting panels for added pattern and visual interest.

c. Picture Frame Molding: Create a more elaborate wainscoting design by adding picture frame molding within the panels for a three-dimensional and sophisticated look.

d. Decorative Inserts: Incorporate decorative inserts, such as carved rosettes, medallions, or inlays, within the wainscoting panels or at the corners of the chair rail for a custom and ornate touch.

By considering these design factors, mastering the installation techniques, and exploring customization options, you can create beautiful and professional-looking wainscoting and chair rail projects that enhance the character, depth, and visual appeal of your interior space. Whether you opt for a classic and traditional look or a more modern and minimalist design, these architectural elements offer a timeless and versatile way to elevate the style and functionality of any room in your home. With the right tools, materials, and creative vision, you can achieve stunning results that reflect your personal taste and showcase your woodworking skills.

Creating Custom Trim Profiles

Custom trim profiles offer a unique and personalized touch to interior woodwork, allowing you to create a one-of-a-kind look that perfectly complements your home's style and character. By designing and crafting your own trim profiles, you can go beyond the standard options available at home improvement stores and create truly distinctive elements that showcase your creativity and woodworking skills. In this section, we'll explore the process of creating custom trim profiles, including the tools and materials needed, the basic steps involved, and some tips and techniques for achieving professional and polished results.

1. Design Considerations

Before creating your custom trim profile, consider the following design factors to ensure a successful and cohesive look:

a. Style and Inspiration: Look for inspiration in architectural styles, historical periods, or existing trim profiles that you admire. Consider the overall style of your home and choose a profile that complements and enhances that aesthetic.

b. Scale and Proportion: Ensure that the scale and proportion of your custom trim profile are appropriate for the size of the room and the dimensions of the walls, doors, or windows it will frame. A trim profile that is too large or too small can look out of place and disrupt the visual balance of the space.

c. Complexity and Skill Level: Assess your woodworking skills and experience when designing your custom trim profile. Start with simpler designs and progressively work towards more complex and intricate profiles as you build your confidence and proficiency.

d. Material and Finish: Choose a wood species and finish that suit your design vision, budget, and durability needs. Consider factors such as grain pattern, color, and how the wood will accept stain or paint when making your selection.

2. Tools and Materials
To create custom trim profiles, you'll need the following tools and materials:

a. Router: A router is the primary tool used for creating custom trim profiles. Choose a router with sufficient power and speed control for your desired profile complexity and wood species.

b. Router Bits: Select router bits that match your desired profile shape and size. Common bit profiles include cove, roundover, ogee, and chamfer, and they come in various sizes and combinations.

c. Router Table (Optional): A router table provides a stable and secure platform for routing longer trim pieces and can help you achieve more consistent and precise results.

d. Wood Stock: Choose straight, dry, and defect-free wood stock in the appropriate dimensions for your trim profile. Popular wood species for trim include pine, poplar, oak, and maple.

e. Measuring and Marking Tools: You'll need a tape measure, pencil, and combination square for accurately measuring and marking the wood stock and trim lengths.

f. Safety Equipment: Always wear appropriate safety gear when working with a router, including eye and ear protection, a dust mask, and sturdy work gloves.

3. Creating the Custom Profile

Follow these steps to create your custom trim profile:

a. Sketch the Profile: Sketch your desired trim profile on paper, including the specific dimensions and shapes of each element. Use a scale ruler or graph paper to ensure accurate proportions.

b. Select the Router Bits: Choose the router bits that most closely match the shapes and sizes of your sketched profile. You may need to use multiple bits to create more complex profiles, routing each section separately.

c. Set Up the Router: Install the selected router bit securely in the router, adjusting the depth and height according to your profile design. If using a router table, ensure that the fence and guard are properly positioned for safety and accuracy.

d. Test the Profile: Before routing your final trim pieces, make test cuts on scrap wood to ensure that the profile matches your design and that the router settings are correct. Adjust as needed until you achieve the desired result.

e. Mill the Trim: With the router set up and tested, mill your trim pieces to the desired lengths, routing the profile along one or more edges as desired. Use a steady and consistent feed rate to ensure a smooth and even profile.

f. Sand and Finish: After routing, sand the trim pieces thoroughly to remove any rough spots or imperfections. Apply your chosen finish, such as stain, paint, or clear coat, according to the manufacturer's instructions.

4. Installation and Customization

Once your custom trim profiles are created, follow these tips for installation and further customization:

a. Measure and Cut: Measure the desired lengths for each trim piece, taking into account the room dimensions and any corner or joint locations. Cut the trim pieces to size using a miter saw, with precise 45-degree angles for mitered corners.

b. Install the Trim: Attach the trim pieces to the walls, doors, or windows using a finish nail gun or hammer, ensuring that the profiles are aligned, level, and tightly fitted at the joints. Fill any nail holes or gaps with wood putty, sand smooth, and touch up the finish as needed.

c. Combine Profiles: For an even more unique and custom look, consider combining different trim profiles within the same room or on the same wall. For example, you could use a larger, more ornate profile for the base molding and a simpler, complementary profile for the chair rail or window casing.

d. Experiment with Scale: Play with the scale and proportion of your custom trim profiles to create visual interest and hierarchy within a room. For example, you could use a larger, bolder profile for a fireplace mantel or a grand entryway, and smaller, more delicate profiles for secondary spaces or transition areas.

e. Incorporate Other Materials: Combine your custom wood trim profiles with other materials, such as metal, stone, or tile, for a unique and eclectic look. For example, you could use a custom wood chair rail with a tiled wainscoting below, or a custom wood casing with a metal inlay or accent.

By mastering the art of creating custom trim profiles, you can take your interior woodworking projects to the next level, adding a truly personalized and distinctive touch to your home's decor. With the right tools, materials, and creative vision, you can design and craft trim profiles that are uniquely suited to your style and space, elevating the overall beauty and character of your home.

Whether you opt for classic and traditional profiles or more modern and minimalist designs, the process of creating custom trim profiles is a rewarding and satisfying endeavor that allows you to showcase your woodworking skills and express your individual taste and creativity.

Chapter 5
Outdoor Woodworking: Building Decks
Planning and Designing Your Dream Deck

Building a deck is an excellent way to extend your living space outdoors and create a beautiful, functional area for relaxing, entertaining, and enjoying the fresh air. A well-designed and constructed deck can add value to your home, increase your outdoor living space, and provide a comfortable and inviting environment for you and your guests. In this section, we'll explore the process of planning and designing your dream deck, including the key considerations, steps, and tips for creating a custom deck that perfectly suits your needs, style, and budget.

Planning and Designing Your Dream Deck

1. Assess Your Space and Needs
Before beginning your deck design, take the time to assess your outdoor space and consider your specific needs and goals for the deck.

a. Location and Size: Determine the ideal location for your deck based on factors such as privacy, sun exposure, and access to the house. Measure the available space and consider the size and shape of the deck that would best fit your needs and complement your home's architecture.

b. Function and Use: Think about how you plan to use your deck and what activities you want to accommodate. Consider factors such as seating areas, dining space, cooking or grilling stations, and recreational features like a hot tub or fire pit.

c. Budget and Materials: Establish a realistic budget for your deck project, taking into account the cost of materials, labor, and any additional features or amenities you wish to include. Research the different decking material options, such as wood, composite, or PVC, and compare their costs, durability, and maintenance requirements.

2. Create a Design Plan

With your space and needs assessed, create a detailed design plan for your deck that includes the following elements:

a. Layout and Floor Plan: Sketch the basic layout and floor plan of your deck, including the dimensions, shape, and placement of key features like stairs, railings, and built-in seating or planters. Use graph paper or a digital design tool to create a scaled drawing of your deck plan.

b. Framing and Structure: Determine the framing and structural elements of your deck, such as the posts, beams, joists, and ledger board. Consider the load-bearing requirements and local building codes when planning your deck's structure, and consult with a professional if needed.

c. Decking and Railing: Choose the decking material and pattern that best suits your style and budget, such as traditional wood boards, composite planks, or interlocking tiles. Select a railing style and material that complements your decking and provides adequate safety and security.

d. Stairs and Access: Plan the location and design of any stairs or access points needed to connect your deck to the ground level or other areas of your yard. Consider factors such as the rise and run of the stairs, the width and placement of the treads, and any necessary landings or handrails.

e. Amenities and Features: Incorporate any desired amenities or special features into your deck design, such as built-in seating, pergolas, lighting, or outdoor kitchens. Consider the placement and integration of these elements within the overall layout and structure of your deck.

3. Obtain Necessary Permits and Approvals

Before beginning construction on your deck, ensure that you have obtained all necessary permits and approvals from your local building department.

a. Building Codes and Regulations: Research and familiarize yourself with the local building codes and regulations that apply to deck construction in your area, including requirements for footings, framing, railings, and stairs.

b. Permit Application: Submit a permit application to your local building department, including your detailed deck plans, materials list, and any required fees or documentation. Be prepared to revise your plans based on feedback or requirements from the building officials.

c. Inspections and Approvals: Schedule any necessary inspections or approvals at key stages of your deck construction, such as after framing, electrical or plumbing work, and final completion. Ensure that your deck meets all required codes and standards before proceeding with each stage of the project.

4. Plan for Utilities and Landscaping

As part of your deck planning process, consider any necessary utility connections or landscaping modifications that may be required.

a. Electrical and Lighting: Plan for any electrical needs, such as outlets or lighting fixtures, and ensure that your deck design includes the necessary wiring and conduit placements. Hire a licensed electrician to handle any complex or high-voltage work.

b. Plumbing and Gas: If your deck will include features like an outdoor kitchen or gas fire pit, plan for the necessary plumbing and gas line connections, and ensure that your design accommodates these elements safely and efficiently.

c. Landscaping and Drainage: Consider the impact of your deck on the surrounding landscaping and plan for any necessary modifications, such as grading, drainage, or plant removal. Ensure that your deck design allows for proper water runoff and does not create any potential drainage or erosion issues.

5. Gather Materials and Tools
With your deck design and permits in place, gather all the necessary materials and tools needed for your project.

a. Materials List: Create a detailed materials list based on your deck plans, including the lumber, hardware, fasteners, and any specialty items like railings, stairs, or decking materials. Order or purchase your materials in advance to avoid delays during construction.

b. Tools and Equipment: Assemble the necessary tools and equipment for your deck build, such as saws, drills, levels, hammers, and safety gear. Rent or purchase any specialty tools or heavy equipment, like a post hole digger or concrete mixer, as needed.

c. Delivery and Storage: Arrange for the delivery and storage of your materials on-site, taking into account factors like weather protection, organization, and accessibility. Ensure that your materials are properly stacked, covered, and secured to prevent damage or theft.

By carefully planning and designing your dream deck, you can create a beautiful and functional outdoor living space that perfectly suits your needs, style, and budget. With a detailed design plan, necessary permits and approvals, and the right materials and tools, you'll be well-prepared to tackle the construction phase of your deck project with confidence and efficiency. Whether you opt for a simple, classic design or a more elaborate, custom creation, the process of planning and designing your dream deck is a rewarding and exciting endeavor that will pay off in years of outdoor enjoyment and satisfaction.

Selecting the Right Materials for Durability

Choosing the right materials for your deck is crucial for ensuring its long-term durability, performance, and aesthetic appeal. With so many options available, from traditional wood to modern composites and synthetics, it's important to carefully consider the unique properties, benefits, and drawbacks of each material before making a decision. In this section, we'll explore the key factors to consider when selecting the right materials for your deck's durability, including the specific characteristics and performance of different decking options, as well as tips for making an informed and confident choice.

1. Understanding Decking Material Options

To select the right materials for your deck's durability, it's important to first understand the various decking options available and their unique properties.

a. Wood: Traditional wood decking, such as pressure-treated pine, cedar, or redwood, offers a classic and natural look, but requires regular maintenance, such as staining, sealing, and cleaning, to prevent weathering, warping, and decay.

b. Composite: Composite decking, made from a blend of wood fibers and plastic polymers, provides a low-maintenance and durable alternative to wood, with improved resistance to moisture, insects, and fading. However, composite decking may lack the natural texture and variations of real wood.

c. PVC: PVC decking, made from 100% synthetic materials, offers superior durability and resistance to moisture, stains, and fading, with minimal maintenance requirements. However, PVC decking may have a more artificial or plastic appearance compared to wood or composites.

d. Aluminum: Aluminum decking, made from lightweight and corrosion-resistant metal, provides a modern and sleek look, with excellent durability and low maintenance needs. However, aluminum decking may be more expensive and have a less traditional appearance than wood or composites.

2. Evaluating Durability Factors

When selecting materials for your deck's durability, consider the following key factors that can impact the long-term performance and longevity of your decking:

a. Moisture Resistance: Evaluate the material's ability to resist moisture, humidity, and water damage, which can cause warping, cupping, or rot in wood decking. Look for materials with inherent moisture resistance or protective coatings.

b. Insect and Decay Resistance: Consider the material's resistance to insect infestations, such as termites or carpenter bees, as well as fungal decay or rot. Choose materials with natural or chemical treatments that repel insects and prevent decay.

c. UV and Fade Resistance: Assess the material's ability to withstand UV radiation and resist fading or discoloration over time. Look for materials with built-in UV inhibitors or protective finishes that maintain color and appearance.

d. Scratch and Stain Resistance: Evaluate the material's resistance to scratches, scuffs, and stains from foot traffic, furniture, or spills. Consider materials with harder surfaces or protective coatings that minimize visible wear and tear.

e. Structural Stability: Assess the material's structural stability and ability to resist warping, cupping, or sagging over time, particularly in response to temperature changes or heavy loads. Look for materials with engineered or reinforced construction for improved stability.

3. Climate and Environmental Considerations
When selecting materials for your deck's durability, it's important to consider the specific climate and environmental factors that can impact the performance and longevity of your decking.

a. Temperature Variations: Evaluate the material's ability to withstand extreme temperature variations, particularly in regions with hot summers or cold winters. Look for materials with good thermal stability and minimal expansion or contraction.

b. Humidity and Moisture: Consider the humidity and moisture levels in your region, particularly if your deck is near a pool, spa, or coastal area. Choose materials with excellent moisture resistance and drainage capabilities to prevent water damage or mold growth.

c. Sun Exposure: Assess the amount and intensity of sun exposure your deck will receive, particularly if it's in a south-facing or unshaded area. Look for materials with good UV resistance and color retention to minimize fading or degradation over time.

d. Environmental Impact: Consider the environmental impact of your decking material choice, particularly in terms of sustainability, recyclability, and carbon footprint. Look for materials with recycled content, low-emission manufacturing processes, or sustainable sourcing practices.

4. Maintenance and Upkeep Requirements

When selecting materials for your deck's durability, it's important to consider the ongoing maintenance and upkeep requirements of each option, and choose a material that aligns with your lifestyle and preferences.

a. Cleaning and Washing: Evaluate the material's ease of cleaning and resistance to dirt, grime, or stains. Consider the frequency and intensity of cleaning required to maintain the material's appearance and performance.

b. Staining and Sealing: Assess the need for regular staining, sealing, or painting to protect the material from moisture, UV damage, or fading. Consider the time, cost, and effort required for these maintenance tasks.

c. Repairs and Replacements: Evaluate the material's ease of repair or replacement in case of damage, wear, or aging. Consider the availability and cost of replacement boards or components, as well as the complexity of the repair process.

d. Long-Term Durability: Assess the material's expected lifespan and long-term durability based on manufacturer warranties, independent testing, or real-world performance data. Consider the potential costs and benefits of investing in a higher-quality or longer-lasting material.

5. Budget and Cost Considerations

When selecting materials for your deck's durability, it's important to consider the overall budget and cost implications of each option, and choose a material that provides the best value and performance for your investment.

a. Initial Costs: Evaluate the upfront costs of each decking material option, including the price per square foot, as well as any additional costs for fasteners, accessories, or specialty tools required for installation.

b. Maintenance Costs: Assess the ongoing costs of maintaining each decking material, including the cost of cleaning supplies, stains, sealants, or repairs over the life of the deck.

c. Long-Term Value: Consider the long-term value and return on investment of each decking material, taking into account factors such as durability, lifespan, and potential impact on home resale value.

d. Warranty and Support: Evaluate the warranty coverage and customer support offered by each decking material manufacturer, including the length and terms of the warranty, as well as the availability of technical support or installation guidance.

By carefully considering these key factors and evaluating the unique properties and performance of different decking material options, you can select the right materials for your deck's durability, ensuring a long-lasting, low-maintenance, and beautiful outdoor living space. Whether you opt for traditional wood, modern composites, or innovative synthetics, the process of selecting the right materials for your deck is a critical step in creating a durable and enjoyable outdoor oasis that will stand the test of time.

Step-by-Step Deck Construction Guide

Building a deck can be a rewarding and challenging project that requires careful planning, preparation, and execution. By following a step-by-step construction guide, you can ensure that your deck is built safely, efficiently, and to the highest standards of quality and durability. In this section, we'll provide a detailed, structured, and in-depth explanation of the key steps involved in constructing a deck, from laying the foundation to adding the finishing touches.

1. Preparing the Site

Before beginning construction, it's important to properly prepare the site for your deck, ensuring a stable and level foundation.

a. Clearing and Grading: Clear the area where your deck will be built of any vegetation, debris, or obstacles. Grade the soil to create a level and well-draining surface, using a laser level or transit to ensure accuracy.

b. Marking and Excavating: Mark the locations of your deck's footings, posts, and perimeter using stakes and string lines. Excavate the footing holes to the required depth and diameter, based on your local building codes and soil conditions.

c. Installing Footings: Pour concrete footings for your deck's posts, ensuring that they are level, plumb, and aligned with your string lines. Allow the footings to cure fully before proceeding with construction.

2. Framing the Deck

With the site prepared and footings in place, you can begin framing the structure of your deck, including the posts, beams, and joists.

a. Installing Posts: Cut your deck posts to the required height and attach them to the footings using post anchors or brackets. Ensure that the posts are plumb and securely fastened.

b. Attaching Beams: Cut and install the deck beams, which will support the joists and decking. Attach the beams to the posts using hardware such as joist hangers or carriage bolts, ensuring that they are level and properly spaced.

c. Installing Joists: Cut and install the deck joists, which will support the decking boards. Attach the joists to the beams using joist hangers, ensuring that they are perpendicular to the beams and spaced according to your decking material and local building codes.

d. Adding Blocking and Bridging: Install blocking and bridging between the joists to provide additional support and stability, particularly in areas where the decking will bear heavy loads or foot traffic.

3. Installing the Decking

With the framing complete, you can begin installing the decking material, which will form the visible surface of your deck.

a. Laying Out the Decking: Begin laying out your decking boards, starting at one end of the deck and working towards the other. Use spacers to ensure consistent gaps between the boards, and stagger the joints for a more attractive and stable surface.

b. Cutting and Fitting: Cut the decking boards to fit around posts, corners, or obstacles, using a circular saw or jigsaw. Ensure that the cuts are clean and precise, and that the boards fit snugly against each other and the framing.

c. Fastening the Decking: Fasten the decking boards to the joists using screws, nails, or hidden fasteners, depending on your decking material and preferences. Ensure that the fasteners are properly spaced and driven flush with the surface of the boards.

d. Trimming and Finishing: Trim any overhanging decking boards using a circular saw or router, ensuring a clean and even edge. Sand any rough spots or splinters, and apply any necessary finishing treatments, such as stain, sealer, or paint.

4. Installing Railings and Stairs
If your deck requires railings or stairs, you'll need to install these elements to ensure safety and accessibility.

a. Attaching Railing Posts: Install the railing posts, ensuring that they are plumb, secure, and spaced according to your local building codes. Attach the posts to the deck framing using bolts, anchors, or brackets.

b. Installing Railing Sections: Cut and install the railing sections between the posts, ensuring that they are level, straight, and properly spaced. Use balusters, pickets, or glass panels to fill in the gaps between the top and bottom rails.

c. Building Stairs: If your deck requires stairs, build them according to your local building codes and the rise and run requirements for your specific height and depth. Ensure that the stairs are properly supported, with stringers, treads, and risers securely fastened.

d. Adding Handrails: Install handrails on your stairs and railings, ensuring that they are the proper height, diameter, and spacing for safety and accessibility. Attach the handrails to the posts or walls using brackets or anchors.

5. Finishing and Maintaining Your Deck

With your deck construction complete, you can add the finishing touches and establish a maintenance routine to keep your deck looking and performing its best.

a. Adding Lighting and Electrical: If desired, install lighting fixtures, outlets, or other electrical features on your deck, following all local codes and safety guidelines. Hire a licensed electrician for any complex or high-voltage work.

b. Installing Landscaping and Drainage: Add any necessary landscaping or drainage features around your deck, such as gravel, plants, or gutters, to ensure proper water management and aesthetic appeal.

c. Cleaning and Maintenance: Establish a regular cleaning and maintenance routine for your deck, including sweeping, washing, and inspecting the surface and structure for any signs of wear, damage, or decay. Follow the manufacturer's recommendations for your specific decking material.

d. Enjoying Your Outdoor Space: Finally, add any desired furniture, accessories, or decor to your deck, and enjoy your beautiful and functional outdoor living space with family and friends.

By following this step-by-step deck construction guide, you can build a strong, durable, and attractive deck that will provide years of outdoor enjoyment and value to your home. Whether you're a seasoned DIYer or a first-time builder, the process of constructing a deck requires careful attention to detail, safety, and craftsmanship, but the end result is a rewarding and satisfying accomplishment that will enhance your home and lifestyle.

Railing and Stair Installation

Installing railings and stairs is a critical aspect of deck construction that ensures the safety, accessibility, and aesthetic appeal of your outdoor living space. Properly designed and installed railings and stairs not only provide necessary support and guidance but also enhance the overall look and functionality of your deck. In this section, we'll provide a detailed, structured, and in-depth explanation of the key considerations and steps involved in installing railings and stairs for your deck.

1. Planning and Design

Before installing railings and stairs, it's important to carefully plan and design these elements to ensure compliance with local building codes and to achieve the desired look and functionality.

a. Building Code Requirements: Familiarize yourself with the local building codes and regulations regarding railing and stair dimensions, spacing, and load-bearing requirements. Ensure that your design meets or exceeds these standards for safety and compliance.

b. Railing Style and Material: Choose a railing style and material that complements your deck's design and enhances its visual appeal. Consider options such as wood, metal, glass, or composite, and select a style that fits your aesthetic preferences and maintenance needs.

c. Stair Layout and Dimensions: Determine the layout and dimensions of your stairs based on the height and location of your deck, as well as the available space and desired access points. Calculate the rise and run of each step to ensure comfortable and safe use, and plan for any necessary landings or turns.

2. Preparing the Structure

With your railing and stair design in place, you can begin preparing the deck structure for installation.

a. Marking and Cutting Posts: Mark the locations of your railing posts on the deck framing, ensuring that they are evenly spaced and aligned with the deck's edge. Cut the posts to the required height, taking into account the height of the railing and the thickness of the decking material.

b. Installing Post Anchors: Install post anchors or brackets on the deck framing at each marked location, ensuring that they are level, plumb, and securely fastened. Use corrosion-resistant hardware and follow the manufacturer's instructions for proper installation.

c. Attaching Stair Stringers: If installing stairs, cut and attach the stair stringers to the deck framing and the ground or landing below. Ensure that the stringers are properly spaced, level, and secured using bolts, hangers, or anchors.

3. Installing Railing Posts

With the structure prepared, you can begin installing the railing posts, which will support the top and bottom rails and the infill material.

a. Setting the Posts: Place the railing posts into the anchors or brackets, ensuring that they are plumb, level, and aligned with the deck's edge. Use shims or spacers to make any necessary adjustments, and secure the posts using bolts, screws, or nails.

b. Cutting and Capping: Cut the tops of the posts to the required height, ensuring a consistent and level surface for the top rail. If desired, add post caps or finials to the tops of the posts for a finished and decorative look.

c. Attaching Stair Posts: If installing stairs, attach the stair railing posts to the stringers using brackets or bolts, ensuring that they are plumb, level, and aligned with the stair treads. Follow the same process for cutting and capping the stair posts.

4. Installing Railing Sections

With the posts in place, you can begin installing the railing sections, which consist of the top and bottom rails and the infill material.

a. Measuring and Cutting Rails: Measure the distance between each set of posts and cut the top and bottom rails to the required length, ensuring a tight and secure fit. If using wood rails, make any necessary miter or bevel cuts for a seamless and attractive joint.

b. Attaching Rails to Posts: Attach the top and bottom rails to the posts using brackets, screws, or nails, ensuring that they are level, parallel, and properly spaced. If using metal or composite rails, follow the manufacturer's instructions for proper assembly and installation.

c. Installing Infill Material: Install the infill material between the top and bottom rails, using pickets, balusters, or panels, depending on your chosen style and material. Ensure that the infill is properly spaced, secured, and aligned for a consistent and attractive appearance.

5. Installing Stair Treads and Risers

If installing stairs, you'll need to install the stair treads and risers, which form the walking surface and vertical face of each step.

a. Cutting and Fitting Treads: Cut the stair treads to the required width and depth, ensuring a consistent overhang and spacing between each tread. If using wood, make any necessary miter or bevel cuts for a tight and seamless fit. If using composite or metal treads, follow the manufacturer's instructions for proper installation.

b. Attaching Treads to Stringers: Attach the stair treads to the stringers using screws, nails, or hidden fasteners, ensuring that they are level, secure, and properly spaced. Use corrosion-resistant hardware and predrill any necessary holes to prevent splitting or cracking.

c. Installing Risers: If desired, install risers between each set of treads to conceal the gaps and create a finished look. Cut the risers to the required height and width, and attach them to the backs of the treads using screws, nails, or adhesive.

6. Adding Finishing Touches

With your railings and stairs installed, you can add the finishing touches to enhance their appearance and durability.

a. Sanding and Finishing: If using wood railings or stairs, sand any rough spots or edges, and apply any necessary stain, sealer, or paint to protect the wood and enhance its color and grain. If using composite or metal, follow the manufacturer's recommendations for cleaning and finishing.

b. Installing Lighting: If desired, install lighting fixtures on your railings or stairs to improve visibility and ambiance. Use low-voltage or solar-powered options for easy installation and energy efficiency, and ensure that the fixtures are properly secured and weatherproofed.

c. Adding Accessories: Consider adding accessories such as railing planters, post caps, or decorative brackets to personalize your railings and stairs and enhance their visual appeal. Ensure that any accessories are properly secured and compatible with your chosen materials.

By following these steps and considerations for installing railings and stairs, you can create a safe, attractive, and functional deck that meets your specific needs and enhances your outdoor living experience. Whether you opt for traditional wood, modern composite, or sleek metal, the process of installing railings and stairs requires careful planning, attention to detail, and a commitment to quality and craftsmanship. With the right tools, materials, and techniques, you can install railings and stairs that will provide lasting beauty, safety, and enjoyment for years to come.

Deck Maintenance and Weatherproofing

Proper maintenance and weatherproofing are essential for ensuring the longevity, durability, and aesthetic appeal of your deck. Regular upkeep not only prevents costly repairs and replacements but also enhances the safety and enjoyment of your outdoor living space. In this section, we'll provide a detailed, structured, and in-depth explanation of the key steps and considerations involved in maintaining and weatherproofing your deck.

1. Cleaning and Inspection

The first step in deck maintenance is regular cleaning and inspection to identify and address any issues before they worsen.

a. Sweeping and Debris Removal: Regularly sweep your deck to remove dust, leaves, and other debris that can trap moisture and promote mold or mildew growth. Pay particular attention to corners, crevices, and areas around furniture or planters.

b. Washing and Scrubbing: Use a garden hose, pressure washer, or deck cleaning solution to remove dirt, grime, and stains from the surface of your deck. For tough stains or mildew, use a stiff-bristled brush or scrub pad, and avoid using excessive pressure that can damage the wood fibers.

c. Rinsing and Drying: Thoroughly rinse your deck with clean water to remove any remaining cleaning solution or debris, and allow the surface to dry completely before applying any treatments or sealers.

d. Inspection and Repair: While cleaning, inspect your deck for any signs of damage, such as warped, cracked, or splintered boards, loose or corroded fasteners, or pest infestations. Make any necessary repairs or replacements promptly to prevent further deterioration.

2. Sanding and Refinishing

Over time, your deck's surface may become rough, discolored, or worn, requiring sanding and refinishing to restore its appearance and protect the wood.

a. Preparation and Safety: Before sanding, remove any furniture, planters, or accessories from your deck, and cover any nearby plants or surfaces to protect them from dust and debris. Wear appropriate safety gear, such as a dust mask, eye protection, and gloves.

b. Sanding and Smoothing: Use a power sander or sandpaper to remove any rough spots, splinters, or raised grain from the surface of your deck. Start with a coarse grit and progress to a finer grit for a smooth and even finish. Sand in the direction of the wood grain, and avoid applying excessive pressure that can create gouges or unevenness.

c. Cleaning and Dust Removal: After sanding, use a broom, vacuum, or leaf blower to remove any dust or debris from the surface of your deck. Ensure that the surface is clean and dry before applying any stain, sealer, or paint.

d. Staining and Sealing: If desired, apply a penetrating stain or sealer to the surface of your deck to enhance its color, grain, and protection against moisture and UV damage. Follow the manufacturer's instructions for application, drying time, and recoat intervals, and avoid applying in direct sunlight or extreme temperatures.

3. Weatherproofing and Protection

Weatherproofing your deck is crucial for protecting it against the elements and extending its lifespan.

a. Water Resistance and Drainage: Ensure that your deck has proper drainage and water resistance to prevent moisture damage and rot. Install flashing or drip edges around the perimeter of your deck, and use water-resistant materials, such as pressure-treated wood or composite, for the decking and framing.

b. UV Protection and Fading: Protect your deck against sun damage and fading by applying a UV-resistant stain, sealer, or paint. Look for products with added pigments or UV inhibitors, and reapply as needed based on the manufacturer's recommendations and your deck's exposure level.

c. Mold and Mildew Prevention: Prevent mold and mildew growth on your deck by ensuring proper ventilation and airflow underneath the decking, and by using mold-resistant materials or treatments. Regularly clean your deck to remove any organic debris or standing water that can promote mold growth.

d. Pest and Insect Control: Protect your deck against pest and insect infestations by using naturally resistant wood species, such as cedar or redwood, or by applying insecticide treatments or barriers. Regularly inspect your deck for any signs of damage or activity, and address any issues promptly with the appropriate control measures.

4. Seasonal Maintenance and Care
Adapt your deck maintenance and weatherproofing routine to the changing seasons and weather conditions to ensure year-round protection and performance.

a. Spring Cleaning and Preparation: In the spring, thoroughly clean and inspect your deck to remove any accumulated dirt, debris, or damage from the winter months. Make any necessary repairs or replacements, and apply any stains, sealers, or treatments before the peak outdoor season.

b. Summer Use and Protection: During the summer, protect your deck from heavy foot traffic, spills, and UV damage by using outdoor rugs, furniture pads, and shade structures. Regularly sweep and rinse your deck to prevent debris buildup, and reapply any protective coatings as needed.

c. Fall Preparation and Cleaning: In the fall, prepare your deck for the colder months by removing any furniture, accessories, or debris, and giving it a thorough cleaning and inspection. Make any necessary repairs or treatments, and cover or store any vulnerable elements to protect them from harsh winter conditions.

d. Winter Protection and Monitoring: During the winter, monitor your deck for any signs of damage or wear from snow, ice, or freezing temperatures. Use a plastic shovel or broom to remove any accumulated snow, and avoid using metal tools or harsh de-icing chemicals that can damage the wood. Consider covering or sealing any exposed areas to prevent moisture infiltration and freeze-thaw cycles.

5. Professional Inspection and Maintenance

While regular DIY maintenance and weatherproofing can go a long way in preserving your deck, it's also important to have your deck professionally inspected and serviced periodically to ensure its safety, stability, and longevity.

a. Annual or Biennial Inspection: Schedule an annual or biennial inspection with a qualified deck professional to assess the overall condition and safety of your deck. They can identify any potential issues or hazards, such as structural damage, fastener corrosion, or code violations, and recommend appropriate repairs or upgrades.

b. Professional Cleaning and Refinishing: Consider hiring a professional deck cleaning and refinishing service every few years to restore the appearance and protection of your deck. They have the tools, expertise, and products to thoroughly clean, sand, and refinish your deck, saving you time and effort while ensuring a high-quality result.

c. Structural Repairs and Reinforcement: If your deck requires significant structural repairs or reinforcement, such as replacing rotted framing, upgrading fasteners, or adding support beams, it's best to hire a licensed and experienced contractor to ensure the work is done safely and correctly. They can also advise you on any necessary permits or code requirements for your area.

d. Warranty and Maintenance Records: Keep records of any professional inspections, repairs, or maintenance performed on your deck, as well as any manufacturer warranties or care instructions for your decking materials or products. This documentation can be valuable for troubleshooting issues, planning future maintenance, or even selling your home.

By following these steps and considerations for deck maintenance and weatherproofing, you can protect your investment, extend the lifespan of your deck, and ensure a safe and enjoyable outdoor living experience for years to come. Whether you have a wood, composite, or metal deck, regular cleaning, inspection, and protection are essential for preventing costly repairs and replacements, while enhancing the beauty and functionality of your outdoor space. With the right tools, products, and techniques, you can maintain and weatherproof your deck like a pro, and enjoy the rewards of a well-cared-for and inviting outdoor retreat.

Chapter 6
Advanced Carpentry Techniques
Creating Inlays and Veneers

As you progress in your woodworking journey, you may want to explore more advanced carpentry techniques that allow you to create intricate, detailed, and unique pieces. Two such techniques are creating inlays and veneers, which involve incorporating contrasting woods or materials into your projects for decorative effect. In this section, we'll provide a detailed, structured, and in-depth explanation of the processes and considerations involved in creating inlays and veneers.

Creating Inlays

Inlays are decorative elements that are set into the surface of a woodworking piece, creating a contrast in color, texture, or material. Inlays can range from simple geometric shapes to complex designs or images and can be made from various materials such as wood, metal, shell, or stone.

1. Designing and Planning

a. Choose a design that complements the overall style and function of your piece. Consider the size, shape, and placement of the inlay, as well as the colors and materials that will create the desired effect.

b. Create a template or pattern for your inlay using paper, cardboard, or thin wood. Ensure that the template is accurately sized and shaped, and that it accounts for the thickness of your inlay material.

2. Preparing the Materials

a. Select the wood or material for your inlay, ensuring that it is thin enough to sit flush with the surface of your piece. Common inlay materials include contrasting wood species, brass, aluminum, shell, or stone.

b. Cut the inlay material to the desired shape and size using a scroll saw, fret saw, or jeweler's saw. For more intricate designs, you may need to use a combination of tools and techniques, such as drilling, filing, or sanding.

3. Cutting the Recess

a. Transfer your inlay template to the surface of your woodworking piece, using a sharp pencil or knife to trace the outline.

b. Use a router or chisel to carefully remove the wood within the outlined area, creating a recess for your inlay. Ensure that the recess is deep enough to accommodate the thickness of your inlay material, and that the edges are clean and square.

4. Fitting and Gluing

a. Test-fit your inlay into the recess, making any necessary adjustments to ensure a snug and flush fit. Use a file, sandpaper, or chisel to fine-tune the shape and size of the inlay or recess as needed.

b. Apply a thin layer of wood glue to the back of the inlay and the bottom of the recess, and carefully place the inlay into position. Use clamps or weights to hold the inlay in place while the glue dries, ensuring that it remains flush and level with the surface.

5. Finishing and Polishing

a. Once the glue has fully dried, use a sharp chisel or scraper to remove any excess glue or inlay material from the surface of your piece. Work carefully to avoid damaging the surrounding wood or the inlay itself.

b. Sand the surface of your piece smoothly, progressively moving from coarser to finer grits until the inlay is flush and the surface is even. Finish your piece with your desired stain, oil, or varnish, taking care to protect and enhance the beauty of the inlay.

Creating Veneers

Veneers are thin sheets of wood that are applied to the surface of a substrate, such as plywood or MDF, to create a decorative and durable finish. Veneers allow you to showcase the beauty of exotic or expensive woods without the cost or weight of solid lumber and can be used to create intricate patterns or designs.

1. Selecting and Preparing the Veneer

a. Choose a veneer species and grain pattern that complements the style and function of your piece. Consider factors such as color, figure, and durability when making your selection.

b. Cut the veneer to the desired size and shape using a sharp utility knife or veneer saw, leaving a slight overhang on all sides to allow for trimming. If using multiple veneer sheets, ensure that the grain patterns and colors match or coordinate as desired.

2. Preparing the Substrate

a. Select a substrate material that is stable, flat, and suitable for your project. Common substrates include plywood, MDF, or particle board, and should be chosen based on factors such as strength, weight, and cost.

b. Cut the substrate to the desired size and shape, and sand the surface smoothly to remove any imperfections or irregularities. Ensure that the substrate is clean, dry, and free of dust or debris before applying the veneer.

3. Applying the Adhesive

a. Choose an adhesive that is compatible with your veneer and substrate materials, and that provides a strong, durable bond. Common adhesives include contact cement, PVA glue, or two-part epoxy.

b. Apply the adhesive evenly to the surface of the substrate and the back of the veneer, using a roller, brush, or spreader. Follow the manufacturer's instructions for application and drying time, and ensure that the adhesive is applied smoothly and consistently.

4. Pressing and Trimming

a. Carefully place the veneer onto the substrate, aligning the edges and corners and smoothing out any air bubbles or wrinkles. Use a veneer roller or press to apply even pressure across the surface, ensuring that the veneer is firmly bonded to the substrate.

b. Allow the adhesive to dry completely, following the manufacturer's recommended time and conditions. Once the adhesive is fully cured, use a sharp utility knife or veneer saw to trim the overhanging edges of the veneer, creating a clean and flush surface.

5. Sanding and Finishing

a. Sand the surface of the veneered piece smoothly, progressively moving from coarser to finer grits until the surface is even and the veneer is fully blended with the substrate. Take care not to sand through the veneer, which can be quite thin and delicate.

b. Finish the veneered surface with your desired stain, oil, or varnish, following the manufacturer's instructions for application and drying time. Consider using a clear or tinted finish that enhances the natural beauty and grain of the veneer, while providing protection against moisture, UV damage, and wear.

By mastering the techniques of creating inlays and veneers, you can add a new level of sophistication, detail, and creativity to your woodworking projects. Whether you're incorporating a simple accent or a complex design, these advanced carpentry techniques allow you to showcase your skills and express your artistic vision in unique and beautiful ways. With practice, patience, and attention to detail, you can create stunning pieces that combine the best of form and function, and that showcase the endless possibilities of working with wood.

Mortise and Tenon Joinery

Mortise and tenon joinery is a classic and strong method for connecting two pieces of wood at a 90-degree angle. This technique has been used for centuries in furniture making, cabinetry, and timber framing, and is known for its strength, durability, and versatility. In this section, we'll provide a detailed, structured, and in-depth explanation of the process and considerations involved in creating mortise and tenon joints.

1. Understanding Mortise and Tenon Joints

a. A mortise is a rectangular cavity cut into the face of one piece of wood, while a tenon is a matching rectangular projection cut on the end of another piece of wood. When the tenon is inserted into the mortise and secured with glue or a fastener, it creates a strong and stable joint.

b. Mortise and tenon joints can be used in a variety of configurations, such as T-joints, L-joints, or cross joints, and can be adapted to different sizes, shapes, and angles depending on the specific application.

2. Tools and Materials

a. Mortising tools: There are several options for cutting mortises, including a dedicated mortising machine, a drill press with a mortising attachment, a router with a straight bit, or hand tools such as a chisel and mallet.

b. Tenoning tools: Tenons can be cut using a table saw with a dado blade, a bandsaw, a handsaw, or a router with a straight bit and a jig.

c. Other tools: You'll also need measuring and marking tools, such as a combination square, marking gauge, and pencil, as well as clamps, a mallet, and a brush for applying glue.

d. Wood: Choose a wood species that is strong, stable, and suitable for your project, such as oak, maple, or cherry. Ensure that the wood is straight, dry, and free of defects or knots that could weaken the joint.

3. Cutting the Mortise

a. Mark the location and size of the mortise on the face of the wood, using a combination square and pencil. The mortise should be centered on the thickness of the wood and should be slightly deeper than the length of the tenon.

b. Set up your chosen mortising tool according to the manufacturer's instructions, ensuring that the bit or chisel is sharp, aligned, and securely fastened.

c. Cut the mortise to the desired depth and width, taking care to keep the sides straight and the bottom flat. Use multiple passes to remove the waste gradually, and check the depth and alignment frequently to ensure accuracy.

d. Clean out any remaining waste or debris from the mortise using a chisel or router, ensuring that the sides are smooth and the corners are square.

4. Cutting the Tenon

a. Mark the location and size of the tenon on the end of the wood, using a combination square and pencil. The tenon should be slightly shorter than the depth of the mortise to allow for glue space, and should have a thickness that is approximately one-third of the thickness of the wood.

b. Set up your chosen tenoning tool according to the manufacturer's instructions, ensuring that the blade or bit is sharp, aligned, and securely fastened.

c. Cut the tenon to the desired length and width, taking care to keep the sides straight and the shoulders square. Use multiple passes to remove the waste gradually, and check the size and fit frequently to ensure accuracy.

d. Test-fit the tenon into the mortise, making any necessary adjustments to ensure a snug and secure fit. The joint should be tight enough to hold together without glue, but not so tight that it requires excessive force to assemble.

5. Gluing and Clamping

a. Apply a thin, even layer of wood glue to the mortise and tenon, using a brush or applicator. Avoid using too much glue, which can weaken the joint or create excess squeeze-out.

b. Insert the tenon into the mortise, aligning the edges and faces of the wood and tapping the joint together with a mallet if necessary. Wipe away any excess glue with a damp cloth before it dries.

c. Clamp the joint securely, using bar clamps, pipe clamps, or other suitable clamping devices. Ensure that the clamps are tightened evenly and that the joint remains square and aligned while the glue dries.

d. Allow the glue to dry completely according to the manufacturer's instructions, which may take several hours or overnight depending on the temperature and humidity conditions.

6. Finishing and Strengthening

a. Once the glue has fully dried, remove the clamps and inspect the joint for any gaps, misalignments, or defects. If necessary, make any final adjustments or repairs using a chisel, saw, or sander.

b. If desired, reinforce the joint with additional fasteners, such as dowels, pins, or screws, which can provide extra strength and stability in high-stress applications. Pre-drill any holes for fasteners to avoid splitting the wood.

c. Sand the joint and surrounding wood smoothly, progressively moving from coarser to finer grits until the surface is even and the joint is flush and seamless. Take care not to round over the edges or corners of the joint, which can weaken its appearance and strength.

d. Finish the wood with your desired stain, oil, or varnish, following the manufacturer's instructions for application and drying time. Consider using a finish that enhances the natural beauty and grain of the wood while providing protection against moisture, UV damage, and wear.

By mastering the technique of mortise and tenon joinery, you can create strong, durable, and attractive connections between pieces of wood that will stand the test of time. Whether you're building furniture, cabinetry, or architectural elements, this classic joint offers a versatile and reliable solution that showcases your skill and craftsmanship. With practice, patience, and attention to detail, you can create mortise and tenon joints that are both functional and beautiful, and that exemplify the best of traditional woodworking techniques.

Dovetail Drawer Construction

Dovetail drawer construction is a classic and highly regarded method for creating strong, durable, and attractive drawers that showcase the skill and craftsmanship of the woodworker. This technique involves cutting interlocking pins and tails on the ends of the drawer front, back, and sides, which fit together like puzzle pieces to create a joint that is both mechanically strong and visually appealing. In this section, we'll provide a detailed, structured, and in-depth explanation of the process and considerations involved in creating dovetail drawers.

1. Understanding Dovetail Joints

a. A dovetail joint consists of two parts: pins, which are narrow, triangular-shaped protrusions cut on the end of one board, and tails, which are wider, triangular-shaped sockets cut on the end of the mating board. When the pins and tails are fitted together, they create a joint that is highly resistant to pulling apart.

b. Dovetail joints can be cut by hand or with a combination of power tools and jigs, and can be customized in terms of the size, spacing, and angle of the pins and tails to suit the specific application and aesthetic preferences of the woodworker.

2. Tools and Materials

a. Dovetailing tools: The most common tools for cutting dovetails include a dovetail saw, which has a thin, flexible blade with fine teeth, and a set of chisels, which are used for cleaning out the waste between the pins and tails. Other useful tools include a marking gauge, a sliding bevel, and a coping saw.

b. Dovetailing jigs: For those who prefer to use power tools, there are several types of dovetailing jigs available that can be used with a router to cut precise, uniform dovetails quickly and easily. These jigs typically include templates for different sizes and styles of dovetails, as well as guides for positioning the workpiece and controlling the depth of cut.

c. Wood: Choose a wood species that is strong, stable, and suitable for drawer construction, such as maple, cherry, or walnut. Ensure that the wood is straight, dry, and free of defects or knots that could weaken the joint.

3. Laying Out the Dovetails

a. Determine the size and spacing of the dovetails based on the dimensions of the drawer and the desired look of the finished piece. A common rule of thumb is to space the pins and tails evenly along the length of the joint, with the pins being narrower than the tails.

b. Mark the location of the pins and tails on the ends of the drawer front, back, and sides using a marking gauge and pencil. Use a sliding bevel to mark the angles of the pins and tails, which are typically set at a ratio of 1:8 or 1:6 (rise to run).

c. Use a dovetail saw to carefully cut along the layout lines, starting with the pins on the drawer front and back, and then transferring their locations to the drawer sides to cut the tails. Take care to keep the saw blade vertical and aligned with the layout lines to ensure a tight, precise fit.

4. Cutting the Pins

a. Secure the drawer front or back in a vise with the end grain facing up, and use a dovetail saw to carefully cut along the layout lines for the pins. Start the saw cut on the waste side of the line and guide the blade with steady, even strokes to maintain a straight, clean cut.

b. Use a coping saw or fret saw to remove the majority of the waste between the pins, being careful not to cut into the layout lines or the pins themselves. Clean up any remaining waste with a sharp chisel, working from both sides of the board to avoid tear-out.

c. Test-fit the pins into the corresponding tails on the drawer side to ensure a snug, precise fit. Make any necessary adjustments with a chisel or saw to fine-tune the fit, taking care not to remove too much material or weaken the joint.

5. Cutting the Tails

a. Transfer the location of the pins to the ends of the drawer sides using a marking knife or pencil, ensuring that the orientation and alignment of the pins are correct. Use a dovetail saw to carefully cut along the transferred lines, starting on the waste side of the line and maintaining a straight, even cut.

b. Remove the waste between the tails using a coping saw or fret saw, being careful not to cut into the layout lines or the tails themselves. Clean up any remaining waste with a sharp chisel, working from both sides of the board to avoid tear-out.

c. Test-fit the tails onto the pins to ensure a snug, precise fit, making any necessary adjustments with a chisel or saw to fine-tune the joint. The goal is to achieve a joint that goes together with light pressure and holds together securely without any gaps or looseness.

6. Gluing and Assembly

a. Dry-fit the drawer components together to ensure that all the joints fit properly and that the drawer is square and aligned. Make any necessary adjustments before proceeding with glue-up.

b. Apply a thin, even layer of wood glue to the mating surfaces of the pins and tails, being careful not to use too much glue, which can weaken the joint or create excessive squeeze-out. Assemble the drawer components, tapping the joints together with a mallet if necessary to ensure a tight, flush fit.

c. Use clamps to secure the drawer while the glue dries, checking for square and adjusting as needed. Wipe away any excess glue with a damp cloth before it dries to avoid interfering with the finish.

d. Allow the glue to dry completely according to the manufacturer's instructions before removing the clamps and proceeding with final sanding and finishing.

7. Finishing and Installation

a. Sand the drawer inside and out to remove any roughness, glue residue, or machining marks, progressively moving from coarser to finer grits until the surface is smooth and even. Take care not to round over the edges or corners of the dovetails, which can weaken their appearance and strength.

b. Apply your desired finish to the drawer, such as stain, oil, or varnish, following the manufacturer's instructions for application and drying time. Consider using a finish that enhances the natural beauty and grain of the wood while providing protection against moisture, wear, and UV damage.

c. Install any necessary hardware, such as drawer slides, pulls, or locks, following the manufacturer's instructions for placement and alignment. Test the operation of the drawer to ensure that it opens and closes smoothly and securely.

d. Mount the drawer in its intended location, such as a cabinet, dresser, or desk, ensuring that it is level, plumb, and aligned with the surrounding components. Make any necessary adjustments to the fit or position of the drawer to achieve optimal functionality and appearance.

By mastering the technique of dovetail drawer construction, you can create drawers that are both beautiful and functional, and that showcase your skill and attention to detail as a woodworker. Whether you're building a single drawer or a full set, this time-honored method offers a strong, durable, and attractive solution that will stand the test of time. With practice, patience, and a commitment to quality craftsmanship, you can create dovetail drawers that are a true testament to your abilities and a source of pride for generations to come.

Crafting Custom Cabinetry

Custom cabinetry is a hallmark of high-end woodworking and a skill that requires a combination of precision, creativity, and attention to detail. Whether you're building kitchen cabinets, bathroom vanities, or built-in storage units, the ability to craft custom cabinetry allows you to create functional and beautiful storage solutions that are tailored to your specific needs and preferences. In this section, we'll provide a detailed, structured, and in-depth explanation of the process and considerations involved in crafting custom cabinetry.

1. Planning and Design

a. Assess the space and storage needs of the room or area where the cabinets will be installed. Take accurate measurements of the available space, including the height, width, and depth of the walls, floors, and ceilings, as well as any obstacles or irregularities that may impact the design.

b. Create a detailed design plan for the cabinets, including the overall layout, dimensions, and style of the units, as well as the specific features and accessories that will be included, such as shelves, drawers, or pullouts. Use sketches, drawings, or computer-aided design (CAD) software to visualize and refine the design.

c. Choose the materials and finishes for the cabinets, taking into account factors such as durability, maintenance, and aesthetics. Common materials for custom cabinetry include solid wood, plywood, MDF, and particleboard, while popular finishes include paint, stain, and varnish.

2. Preparing the Materials

a. Select the lumber or sheet goods for the cabinet boxes, frames, and doors based on the design plan and material choices. Ensure that the wood is straight, flat, and free of defects or imperfections that could affect the strength or appearance of the finished product.

b. Cut the components to size using a table saw, miter saw, or panel saw, taking care to ensure accurate and precise cuts. Label and organize the pieces as they are cut to avoid confusion and errors during assembly.

c. Sand the components thoroughly to remove any roughness, saw marks, or imperfections, progressively moving from coarser to finer grits until the surface is smooth and even. Take care not to round over the edges or corners, which can affect the fit and alignment of the components.

3. Constructing the Cabinet Boxes

a. Assemble the cabinet boxes using the cut and sanded components, following the design plan and joinery methods specified. Common joinery techniques for cabinet boxes include dado joints, rabbet joints, and pocket screws, which provide strong and stable connections between the parts.

b. Install any necessary support structures, such as stretchers, braces, or cleats, to reinforce the cabinet boxes and prevent sagging or movement over time. Ensure that the support structures are level, plumb, and securely fastened to the cabinet boxes.

c. Attach the cabinet boxes to the wall or each other using screws, nails, or other fasteners, taking care to ensure that the units are level, plumb, and aligned with each other and the surrounding walls and floors. Use shims or spacers as needed to accommodate any irregularities or unevenness in the installation area.

4. Installing the Doors and Drawers

a. Measure and cut the components for the cabinet doors and drawer fronts, taking into account the desired style, overlap, and clearance for hinges and pulls. Common styles for cabinet doors include raised panel, recessed panel, and slab, while drawer fronts may be flush, overlaid, or inset.

b. Assemble the doors and drawers using the appropriate joinery methods and hardware, such as cope and stick joints, dowels, or biscuits for the doors, and dovetail or box joints for the drawers. Ensure that the doors and drawers fit properly and operate smoothly within the cabinet openings.

c. Install the hinges, pulls, and other hardware on the doors and drawers, following the manufacturer's instructions for placement and alignment. Adjust the hinges as needed to ensure that the doors hang straight and close securely, and that the drawers slide smoothly and evenly.

5. Finishing and Installation

a. Sand the assembled cabinets, doors, and drawers thoroughly to remove any roughness, glue residue, or machining marks, progressively moving from coarser to finer grits until the surface is smooth and even. Take care not to round over the edges or corners, which can affect the fit and appearance of the finished product.

b. Apply the desired finish to the cabinets, doors, and drawers, such as paint, stain, or varnish, following the manufacturer's instructions for application and drying time. Consider using a finish that enhances the natural beauty and grain of the wood while providing protection against moisture, wear, and UV damage.

c. Install any additional features or accessories, such as shelves, pullouts, or lighting, following the design plan and manufacturer's instructions for placement and operation. Test the function and fit of all components to ensure that they operate smoothly and securely.

d. Mount the finished cabinets in their intended location, ensuring that they are level, plumb, and aligned with the surrounding walls, floors, and ceilings. Use shims or spacers as needed to accommodate any irregularities or unevenness in the installation area, and secure the cabinets to the wall or each other using screws, nails, or other fasteners.

6. Customization and Personalization

a. Consider adding custom features or details to the cabinets to enhance their functionality, style, or personal touch. Examples might include unique hardware, decorative moldings, glass inserts, or special storage solutions like spice racks or wine cubbies.

b. Incorporate the cabinets into the overall design and aesthetic of the room, taking into account factors such as color scheme, lighting, and adjacent materials or finishes. Consider how the cabinets will complement or contrast with other elements in the space, such as countertops, flooring, or wall treatments.

c. Plan for future adaptability or expansion of the cabinets, such as allowing for additional shelves, drawers, or modules to be added as storage needs change over time. Consider using adjustable or removable components that can be easily modified or reconfigured as needed.

d. Personalize the cabinets with meaningful or sentimental elements, such as family photos, heirlooms, or artwork, to create a sense of connection and history within the space. Consider incorporating display areas, niches, or other features that allow for the showcase of personal items or collections.

By mastering the art of crafting custom cabinetry, you can create storage solutions that are both beautiful and functional, and that reflect your unique style, needs, and preferences. Whether you're working on a small renovation or a full-scale remodel, the ability to design and build custom cabinets allows you to make the most of your space and create a truly personalized living environment. With careful planning, skilled execution, and attention to detail, you can craft custom cabinetry that is a true testament to your woodworking abilities and a source of pride and enjoyment for years to come.

120

Chapter 7
Woodworking Projects for Every Room

Kitchen: Cutting Boards and Spice Racks

The kitchen is the heart of the home, and it's also a great place to showcase your woodworking skills with functional and beautiful projects like cutting boards and spice racks. These items not only add a personal touch to your kitchen décor but also serve practical purposes that make meal preparation and cooking more enjoyable and efficient. In this section, we'll provide a detailed, structured, and in-depth explanation of the process and considerations involved in creating cutting boards and spice racks for your kitchen.

Cutting Boards

1. Choosing the Wood

a. Select a hardwood species that is durable, non-porous, and safe for food contact, such as maple, cherry, walnut, or teak. Avoid woods with high toxicity or strong odors, such as red cedar or black locust.

b. Consider the grain pattern and color of the wood, and how it will complement your kitchen décor and personal style. You may also want to mix and match different wood species to create a unique and visually interesting cutting board.

c. Ensure that the wood is properly seasoned and free of defects, such as knots, cracks, or warping, which can affect the strength and longevity of the cutting board.

2. Designing the Cutting Board

a. Determine the size and shape of the cutting board based on your intended use and storage needs. Common sizes range from small (8" x 10") to large (18" x 24"), while shapes can be rectangular, square, or round.

b. Consider adding features or details to the cutting board, such as a juice groove to collect liquids, a handle for easy gripping, or a hanging hole for storage.

c. Sketch or create a digital design of the cutting board, including the dimensions, layout, and any decorative elements or inlays.

3. Preparing the Wood

a. Cut the wood to the desired size and shape using a table saw, miter saw, or band saw, ensuring that the cuts are straight, square, and precise.

b. Plane or sand the wood to a consistent thickness, removing any saw marks or rough spots and creating a smooth, even surface.

c. If creating a cutting board with multiple pieces or a decorative pattern, arrange and glue the pieces together, using clamps to ensure a tight and even bond.

4. Shaping and Finishing

a. Use a router or sandpaper to round over the edges and corners of the cutting board, creating a smooth and comfortable grip and preventing splintering or cracking.

b. Sand the entire cutting board with progressively finer grits of sandpaper, starting with a coarse grit (60-80) and moving up to a fine grit (220-320), until the surface is smooth and free of scratches or blemishes.

c. Apply a food-safe finish to the cutting board, such as mineral oil, beeswax, or a combination of the two, to protect the wood from moisture and bacteria and to enhance its natural beauty and luster.

Spice Racks

1. Assessing Your Spice Collection

a. Take inventory of your spice collection, noting the number, size, and type of containers you have, as well as any specific storage needs or preferences.

b. Consider how you use your spices in the kitchen, and how a spice rack can make them more accessible, organized, and visually appealing.

c. Measure the available space in your kitchen where you want to install the spice rack, taking into account factors such as proximity to the stove, clearance for cabinet doors, and ease of access.

2. Designing the Spice Rack

a. Choose a style and configuration for your spice rack that suits your needs and preferences, such as a wall-mounted shelf, a lazy Susan, a drawer insert, or a countertop carousel.

b. Determine the dimensions and spacing of the spice rack based on your container sizes and the available space in your kitchen.

c. Sketch or create a digital design of the spice rack, including the overall layout, shelving arrangement, and any decorative elements or labels.

3. Selecting the Materials

a. Choose a wood species that is strong, stable, and complementary to your kitchen décor, such as oak, maple, or cherry.

b. Consider using plywood or MDF for the shelves or backing of the spice rack, as these materials are lightweight, affordable, and easy to work with.

c. Select hardware and accessories that are appropriate for the style and function of your spice rack, such as brackets, hinges, or lazy Susan bearings.

4. Constructing the Spice Rack

   a. Cut the wood components to size according to your design plan, using a table saw, miter saw, or circular saw for straight cuts and a jigsaw or band saw for curved cuts.

   b. Assemble the spice rack using wood glue, nails, or screws, ensuring that the joints are square, tight, and secure.

   c. Sand the spice rack thoroughly to remove any rough spots or imperfections, and apply a finish that is appropriate for the wood species and the intended use, such as a clear coat, stain, or paint.

5. Installing and Organizing

   a. Mount the spice rack in your chosen location, using appropriate hardware and anchors to ensure that it is level, plumb, and secure.

   b. Arrange your spice containers on the shelves or in the drawers of the spice rack, grouping them by type, frequency of use, or alphabetical order for easy access and organization.

   c. Consider adding labels or tags to the spice containers or shelves to help identify the contents and expiration dates, and to create a cohesive and attractive display.

By creating custom cutting boards and spice racks for your kitchen, you can add both function and beauty to one of the most important rooms in your home. These projects allow you to showcase your woodworking skills while also creating practical tools that make cooking and meal preparation more enjoyable and efficient. With careful planning, quality materials, and attention to detail, you can craft cutting boards and spice racks that are not only useful but also serve as conversation pieces and cherished family heirlooms for generations to come.

Bathroom: Vanity and Medicine Cabinet

The bathroom is a highly functional and personal space that can benefit greatly from custom woodworking projects like vanities and medicine cabinets. These items not only provide essential storage and organization for toiletries, linens, and other bathroom essentials but also contribute to the overall style and aesthetic of the room. In this section, we'll provide a detailed, structured, and in-depth explanation of the process and considerations involved in creating custom vanities and medicine cabinets for your bathroom.

Vanity

1. Assessing Your Bathroom Space

a. Measure the available space in your bathroom where you want to install the vanity, taking into account factors such as plumbing locations, electrical outlets, and clearance for doors and drawers.

b. Consider the number of sinks, the type of countertop, and the amount of storage you need in your vanity, based on your daily routines and personal preferences.

c. Determine the style and aesthetic of your bathroom, and how the vanity can complement or enhance the overall design, such as through the choice of wood species, hardware, or decorative elements.

2. Designing the Vanity

a. Choose a layout and configuration for your vanity that suits your needs and preferences, such as a freestanding cabinet, a wall-mounted unit, or a corner design.

b. Determine the dimensions and proportions of the vanity based on the available space, the size of your sink(s), and the desired height and depth of the countertop.

c. Sketch or create a digital design of the vanity, including the overall structure, door and drawer placement, and any decorative details or hardware.   **125**

3. Selecting the Materials

   a. Choose a wood species that is durable, moisture-resistant, and complementary to your bathroom décor, such as oak, maple, cherry, or teak.

   b. Consider using plywood or MDF for the carcass or interior of the vanity, as these materials are stable, affordable, and easy to work with.

   c. Select a countertop material that is appropriate for the style and function of your vanity, such as granite, marble, quartz, or solid surface, taking into account factors such as durability, maintenance, and cost.

4. Constructing the Vanity

   a. Build the carcass or frame of the vanity using the chosen wood materials, ensuring that the structure is square, level, and properly supported.

   b. Install the doors, drawers, and hardware according to your design plan, using appropriate joinery techniques and fasteners to ensure smooth and secure operation.

   c. Mount the sink(s) and faucet(s) to the countertop, following the manufacturer's instructions and local plumbing codes for proper installation and sealing.

5. Finishing and Installation

   a. Sand the vanity thoroughly to remove any rough spots or imperfections, and apply a finish that is appropriate for the wood species and the bathroom environment, such as a moisture-resistant stain, paint, or clear coat.

   b. Install the vanity in your bathroom, ensuring that it is level, plumb, and securely fastened to the wall or floor as needed.

   c. Connect the plumbing and electrical components of the vanity, such as the water supply lines, drain pipes, and outlets, following local codes and best practices for safety and functionality.

Medicine Cabinet

1. Assessing Your Storage Needs
a. Take inventory of the items you want to store in your medicine cabinet, such as medications, first aid supplies, toiletries, and grooming tools.

b. Consider the size and quantity of these items, as well as any specific storage requirements, such as temperature control or child safety.

c. Measure the available wall space in your bathroom where you want to install the medicine cabinet, taking into account factors such as mirror placement, lighting, and clearance for the door.

2. Designing the Medicine Cabinet
a. Choose a style and configuration for your medicine cabinet that suits your needs and preferences, such as a recessed, surface-mounted, or corner unit.

b. Determine the dimensions and proportions of the medicine cabinet based on your storage needs and the available wall space, taking into account factors such as shelf spacing and door swing.

c. Sketch or create a digital design of the medicine cabinet, including the overall structure, shelf layout, and any decorative details or hardware.

3. Selecting the Materials
a. Choose a wood species that is stable, moisture-resistant, and complementary to your bathroom décor, such as oak, maple, or poplar.

b. Consider using plywood or MDF for the carcass or shelves of the medicine cabinet, as these materials are lightweight, affordable, and easy to work with.

c. Select a mirror and hardware that are appropriate for the style and function of your medicine cabinet, such as a beveled edge, a adjustable shelves, or a locking mechanism.

4. Constructing the Medicine Cabinet

a. Build the carcass or frame of the medicine cabinet using the chosen wood materials, ensuring that the structure is square, level, and properly supported.

b. Install the shelves, door, and hardware according to your design plan, using appropriate joinery techniques and fasteners to ensure smooth and secure operation.

c. Mount the mirror to the door or back of the medicine cabinet, using a strong adhesive or mechanical fasteners to ensure a secure and level installation.

5. Finishing and Installation

a. Sand the medicine cabinet thoroughly to remove any rough spots or imperfections, and apply a finish that is appropriate for the wood species and the bathroom environment, such as a moisture-resistant paint or clear coat.

b. Install the medicine cabinet in your bathroom, ensuring that it is level, plumb, and securely fastened to the wall studs or blocking as needed.

c. Adjust the shelves and door as needed to ensure proper alignment and smooth operation, and test the locking mechanism (if applicable) to ensure that it engages securely.

By creating custom vanities and medicine cabinets for your bathroom, you can elevate the functionality, organization, and style of this essential space in your home. These projects allow you to tailor the storage and design to your specific needs and preferences, while also showcasing your woodworking skills and creativity. With thoughtful planning, quality materials, and attention to detail, you can craft bathroom vanities and medicine cabinets that are not only practical but also beautiful, adding value and character to your home for years to come.

Bedroom: Headboard and Nightstand

The bedroom is a personal sanctuary where comfort, relaxation, and individual style are paramount. Custom woodworking projects like headboards and nightstands can greatly enhance the functionality and aesthetic of this space, creating a cohesive and inviting atmosphere that reflects your unique tastes and needs. In this section, we'll provide a detailed, structured, and in-depth explanation of the process and considerations involved in creating custom headboards and nightstands for your bedroom.

Headboard

1. Determining Your Style and Needs

a. Consider the overall style and décor of your bedroom, and how the headboard can complement or serve as a focal point for the space, such as through the choice of wood species, shape, or upholstery.

b. Determine the size and proportions of the headboard based on the dimensions of your bed frame and mattress, taking into account factors such as height, width, and thickness.

c. Assess any additional functions or features you want to incorporate into the headboard, such as built-in lighting, storage, or adjustability.

2. Designing the Headboard

a. Choose a design and structure for your headboard that suits your style and needs, such as a solid panel, a slatted frame, or an upholstered cover.

b. Sketch or create a digital design of the headboard, including the overall shape, dimensions, and any decorative details or hardware.

c. Consider the joinery and support methods for the headboard, such as using dowels, biscuits, or metal brackets to connect the components and attach the headboard to the bed frame.

3. Selecting the Materials

a. Choose a wood species that is strong, durable, and complementary to your bedroom décor, such as oak, maple, cherry, or walnut.

b. Consider using plywood or MDF for the core or backing of the headboard, as these materials are stable, affordable, and easy to work with.

c. Select any additional materials needed for the headboard, such as foam padding, fabric, or hardware, based on your design and desired level of comfort and style.

4. Constructing the Headboard

a. Cut the wood components to size according to your design plan, using a table saw, miter saw, or circular saw for straight cuts and a jigsaw or band saw for curved cuts.

b. Assemble the headboard frame using the chosen joinery methods and fasteners, ensuring that the structure is square, level, and properly supported.

c. If upholstering the headboard, attach the foam padding and fabric cover to the frame using adhesive, staples, or tufting techniques, taking care to create a smooth and even surface.

5. Finishing and Installation

a. Sand the headboard thoroughly to remove any rough spots or imperfections, and apply a finish that is appropriate for the wood species and the bedroom environment, such as a stain, paint, or clear coat.

b. Install the headboard on your bed frame, using the appropriate hardware and fasteners to ensure a secure and level attachment.

c. Add any final touches or accessories to the headboard, such as decorative nails, buttons, or trim, to enhance its visual appeal and tie it into the overall bedroom design.

Nightstand

1. Assessing Your Storage and Style Needs

a. Consider the items you want to keep within reach of your bed, such as books, devices, glasses, or a lamp, and how the nightstand can provide convenient and organized storage for these items.

b. Determine the size and proportions of the nightstand based on the available space next to your bed, taking into account factors such as height, width, and depth.

c. Choose a style and aesthetic for the nightstand that complements your bedroom décor and personal tastes, such as a traditional, modern, or rustic design.

2. Designing the Nightstand

a. Decide on the structure and layout of the nightstand, such as the number of drawers, shelves, or compartments, and their placement and dimensions.

b. Sketch or create a digital design of the nightstand, including the overall shape, proportions, and any decorative details or hardware.

c. Consider the joinery and construction methods for the nightstand, such as using dovetails, rabbets, or dadoes to connect the components and ensure structural integrity.

3. Selecting the Materials

a. Choose a wood species that is durable, attractive, and well-suited to the style of your nightstand, such as pine, cherry, or mahogany.

b. Consider using plywood or solid wood for the carcass and drawers of the nightstand, depending on your desired level of strength, stability, and cost-effectiveness.

c. Select any additional materials needed for the nightstand, such as drawer slides, pulls, or locks, based on your design and functional requirements.

4. Constructing the Nightstand

a. Cut the wood components to size according to your design plan, using a table saw, miter saw, or circular saw for precise and accurate cuts.

b. Assemble the nightstand carcass using the chosen joinery methods and fasteners, ensuring that the structure is square, level, and properly aligned.

c. Install the drawers, shelves, and hardware according to your design plan, using appropriate techniques and tools to ensure smooth and secure operation.

5. Finishing and Placement

a. Sand the nightstand thoroughly to remove any rough spots or imperfections, and apply a finish that is appropriate for the wood species and the bedroom environment, such as a stain, paint, or clear coat.

b. Place the nightstand next to your bed, ensuring that it is level, stable, and at a comfortable height for accessing your belongings.

c. Style the nightstand with your chosen items and accessories, such as a lamp, books, or decorative objects, to create a functional and visually appealing bedside vignette.

By creating custom headboards and nightstands for your bedroom, you can infuse this intimate space with your personal style, while also enhancing its comfort, functionality, and organization. These projects allow you to tailor the design and construction to your specific needs and preferences, resulting in pieces that are not only practical but also meaningful and reflective of your unique tastes. With careful planning, quality materials, and skilled craftsmanship, you can create bedroom furnishings that elevate your space and provide a sense of pride and satisfaction every time you retire for the night.

Living Room: Coffee Table and Entertainment Center

The living room is often the central gathering space in a home, where family and friends come together to relax, socialize, and enjoy various forms of entertainment. Custom woodworking projects like coffee tables and entertainment centers can significantly enhance the functionality and aesthetic of this important room, creating a warm and inviting atmosphere that reflects your personal style and meets your specific needs. In this section, we'll provide a detailed, structured, and in-depth explanation of the process and considerations involved in creating custom coffee tables and entertainment centers for your living room.

Coffee Table

1. Determining Your Style and Functional Needs

a. Consider the overall style and décor of your living room, and how the coffee table can complement or serve as a focal point for the space, such as through the choice of wood species, shape, or design elements.

b. Assess the functional requirements for your coffee table, such as the desired size, height, and storage options, based on your living room layout and intended use.

c. Determine any additional features or customization you want to incorporate into the coffee table, such as built-in drawers, shelves, or a lift-top mechanism.

2. Designing the Coffee Table

a. Choose a design and structure for your coffee table that suits your style and functional needs, such as a traditional four-leg table, a modern slab table, or a rustic trunk-style table.

b. Sketch or create a digital design of the coffee table, including the overall shape, dimensions, and any decorative details or hardware.

133

c. Consider the joinery and support methods for the coffee table, such as using mortise and tenon joints, dowels, or metal brackets to connect the components and ensure structural stability.

3. Selecting the Materials

a. Choose a wood species that is durable, attractive, and well-suited to the style of your coffee table, such as oak, walnut, or reclaimed lumber.

b. Consider using solid wood, plywood, or a combination of materials for the tabletop and base, depending on your desired level of strength, stability, and visual appeal.

c. Select any additional materials needed for the coffee table, such as glass inserts, metal accents, or hardware, based on your design and desired aesthetic.

4. Constructing the Coffee Table

a. Cut the wood components to size according to your design plan, using a table saw, miter saw, or circular saw for precise and accurate cuts.

b. Assemble the coffee table base and top using the chosen joinery methods and fasteners, ensuring that the structure is square, level, and properly aligned.

c. Install any additional features or components, such as drawers, shelves, or lift-top hardware, according to your design plan and the manufacturer's instructions.

5. Finishing and Placement

a. Sand the coffee table thoroughly to remove any rough spots or imperfections, and apply a finish that is appropriate for the wood species and the living room environment, such as a stain, paint, or clear coat.

b. Place the coffee table in your living room, ensuring that it is centered and properly positioned in relation to your seating arrangement and other furniture pieces.

c. Style the coffee table with your chosen decor and accessories, such as books, candles, or decorative trays, to create an inviting and cohesive look that ties into the overall living room design.

Entertainment Center

1. Assessing Your Media and Storage Needs
a. Take inventory of your media components, such as your TV, speakers, gaming consoles, and cable boxes, and determine their sizes and placement requirements.

b. Consider your storage needs for media items, such as DVDs, CDs, books, or decorative objects, and how the entertainment center can provide organized and accessible storage solutions.

c. Measure the available space in your living room where you want to install the entertainment center, taking into account factors such as wall dimensions, electrical outlets, and viewing distances.

2. Designing the Entertainment Center
a. Choose a style and configuration for your entertainment center that suits your needs and complements your living room décor, such as a wall-mounted unit, a freestanding cabinet, or a modular system.

b. Determine the dimensions and proportions of the entertainment center based on your media components, storage needs, and available space, taking into account factors such as shelf spacing, drawer sizes, and clearance for doors.

c. Sketch or create a digital design of the entertainment center, including the overall structure, component layout, and any decorative details or hardware.

3. Selecting the Materials

a. Choose a wood species that is strong, durable, and complementary to your living room décor, such as oak, maple, or cherry.

b. Consider using plywood or MDF for the carcass or shelves of the entertainment center, as these materials are stable, affordable, and easy to work with.

c. Select any additional materials needed for the entertainment center, such as tempered glass, metal hardware, or cable management components, based on your design and functional requirements.

4. Constructing the Entertainment Center

a. Build the carcass or frame of the entertainment center using the chosen wood materials, ensuring that the structure is square, level, and properly supported.

b. Install the shelves, drawers, doors, and hardware according to your design plan, using appropriate joinery techniques and fasteners to ensure smooth and secure operation.

c. Integrate any media components, such as the TV mount, speaker brackets, or cable management systems, into the entertainment center, following the manufacturer's instructions and best practices for safety and performance.

5. Finishing and Installation

a. Sand the entertainment center thoroughly to remove any rough spots or imperfections, and apply a finish that is appropriate for the wood species and the living room environment, such as a stain, paint, or clear coat.

b. Install the entertainment center in your living room, ensuring that it is level, plumb, and securely fastened to the wall studs or floor as needed.

c. Connect and organize your media components within the entertainment center, using cable management solutions to minimize clutter and ensure easy access to ports and controls.

By creating custom coffee tables and entertainment centers for your living room, you can elevate the style, functionality, and comfort of this central space in your home. These projects allow you to tailor the design and construction to your specific needs and preferences, resulting in pieces that are not only practical but also reflective of your personal taste and lifestyle. With thoughtful planning, quality materials, and skilled craftsmanship, you can create living room furnishings that become cherished focal points and gathering spots for years to come, enhancing the warmth and enjoyment of your home.

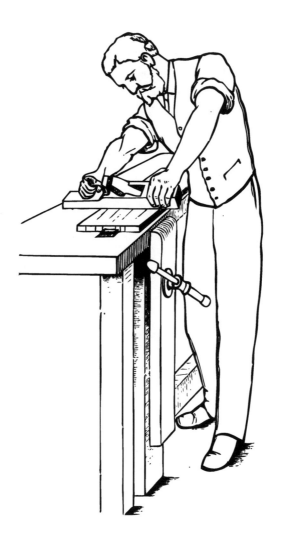

Chapter 8
Troubleshooting and Common Mistakes

Fixing Gaps and Imperfections

Woodworking projects, even those crafted by experienced professionals, are rarely perfect. Gaps, imperfections, and minor flaws are common issues that can arise during the construction process, whether due to variations in wood, inaccuracies in cutting or assembly, or changes in humidity and temperature. However, these issues don't have to detract from the overall quality and appearance of your project. In this section, we'll provide a detailed, structured, and in-depth explanation of the techniques and considerations involved in fixing gaps and imperfections in your woodworking projects.

1. Identifying Gaps and Imperfections
    a. Visually inspect your project for any noticeable gaps, cracks, or misalignments, paying close attention to joints, seams, and transitions between components.
    b. Run your fingers along the surface of the project to feel for any unevenness, roughness, or irregularities that may require attention.
    c. Use a straightedge, square, or level to check for any deviations from the intended shape or alignment of the project, such as warping, twisting, or sagging.

2. Determining the Cause and Severity
    a. Assess the nature and extent of the gap or imperfection, and consider whether it is purely cosmetic or if it affects the structural integrity or functionality of the piece.
    b. Identify the likely cause of the issue, such as wood movement, improper joinery, or machining errors, to inform your approach to fixing it.

c. Evaluate the feasibility and potential impact of attempting to fix the issue, weighing factors such as the time, effort, and materials required, as well as the risk of causing further damage or degrading the overall appearance of the project.

3. Preparing the Area for Repair

a. Clean the affected area thoroughly, removing any dust, debris, or loose material that may interfere with the repair process.

b. If necessary, remove any existing finish, such as paint or stain, from the area surrounding the gap or imperfection to ensure proper adhesion and blending of the repair material.

c. Depending on the nature of the repair, you may need to create a clean, smooth, or slightly roughened surface to promote better bonding or filling of the gap or imperfection.

4. Filling Gaps and Cracks

a. For small gaps and cracks, use a wood filler or putty that closely matches the color and texture of the surrounding wood. Apply the filler with a putty knife or finger, pressing it firmly into the gap to ensure complete coverage.

b. For larger gaps or cracks, consider using a two-part epoxy filler, which provides stronger adhesion and can be tinted or textured to match the surrounding wood. Mix the epoxy according to the manufacturer's instructions and apply it carefully, using a putty knife or syringe to fill the gap completely.

c. If the gap is particularly large or spans a structural joint, you may need to use a more substantial repair method, such as inserting a fitted wood patch or splicing in a new section of wood. Cut the patch or splice to fit the gap precisely, and secure it in place with wood glue and clamps until fully cured.

5. Sanding and Blending

a. Once the filler or repair material has fully dried or cured, use sandpaper to smooth and blend the repair with the surrounding wood. Start with a medium grit (80-120) to remove any excess material and create a flush surface, then progress to finer grits (150-220) to achieve a smooth, seamless transition.

b. If the repair involves a visible patch or splice, carefully shape and contour the edges of the repair to match the grain and profile of the surrounding wood, using chisels, files, or sanding tools as needed.

c. To further blend the repair with the surrounding wood, you may need to apply a stain, dye, or tinted finish to match the color and tone of the original surface. Test the color on a scrap piece of wood first, and apply it carefully to avoid overwetting or creating drips or runs.

6. Addressing Imperfections in Finish

a. If the imperfection is primarily in the finish layer, such as bubbles, brush marks, or uneven coverage, you may be able to correct it by sanding the affected area with fine-grit sandpaper (220-400) and reapplying the finish in thin, even coats.

b. For more severe finish imperfections, such as peeling, cracking, or discoloration, you may need to strip the existing finish completely using a chemical stripper or sanding, then clean and prepare the surface for refinishing.

c. When applying new finish to the repaired area, take care to match the sheen, transparency, and application method of the original finish as closely as possible to ensure a consistent and seamless appearance.

7. Preventing Future Gaps and Imperfections

a. To minimize the occurrence of gaps and imperfections in future projects, take steps to ensure accurate and precise measuring, cutting, and assembly of components, using properly calibrated tools and jigs as needed.

b. Allow wood to acclimate to your workshop environment before cutting and assembling, to reduce the risk of warping, cupping, or bowing due to changes in humidity or temperature.

c. Use appropriate joinery techniques and fasteners for the specific application and wood type, taking into account factors such as grain direction, load-bearing requirements, and seasonal movement.

d. Apply finishes in a controlled environment with proper ventilation, temperature, and humidity, following the manufacturer's instructions for application, drying, and curing times to ensure a smooth, even, and durable surface.

By understanding the techniques and considerations involved in fixing gaps and imperfections in your woodworking projects, you can address these common issues with confidence and skill, resulting in pieces that look and perform their best. Whether you're dealing with minor cosmetic flaws or more significant structural challenges, the key is to approach the repair process methodically, using the appropriate tools, materials, and techniques for the specific situation. With practice and attention to detail, you can develop the ability to seamlessly blend repairs and imperfections into the overall beauty and craftsmanship of your woodworking projects.

Preventing Wood Warping and Splitting

Wood is a natural, organic material that is susceptible to changes in shape and structure due to variations in moisture content and environmental conditions. Two common issues that can arise in woodworking projects are warping and splitting, which can compromise the stability, functionality, and appearance of the finished piece. In this section, we'll provide a detailed, structured, and in-depth explanation of the causes, prevention, and mitigation strategies for wood warping and splitting.

1. Understanding Wood Movement

a. Wood is a hygroscopic material, meaning it naturally absorbs and releases moisture from the surrounding environment, causing it to expand and contract as the humidity changes.

b. The degree and direction of wood movement vary depending on the species, grain orientation, and cut of the lumber, with some woods being more stable than others.

c. Warping refers to the distortion of a piece of wood from its original, intended shape, and can manifest as cupping (curved across the width), bowing (curved along the length), or twisting (spiraled along the length).

d. Splitting occurs when the wood fibers separate along the grain, often due to rapid or uneven changes in moisture content, which create internal stresses that exceed the strength of the wood.

2. Factors Contributing to Warping and Splitting

a. Moisture Content: The primary cause of wood movement is changes in moisture content, which can be influenced by humidity, temperature, and exposure to water or other liquids.

b. Grain Orientation: The direction and alignment of the wood fibers, or grain, can affect how the wood moves and how prone it is to warping or splitting. Quarter-sawn and rift-sawn lumber tend to be more stable than plain-sawn lumber.

c. Species Characteristics: Different wood species have varying degrees of natural stability, with some woods being more resistant to movement and deformation than others. For example, mahogany and teak are known for their stability, while beech and hickory are more prone to movement.

d. Milling and Drying: The way the lumber is cut, processed, and dried can also influence its stability and tendency to warp or split. Proper kiln-drying and acclimation of the wood before use can help minimize movement and defects.

3. Preventing Warping and Splitting in Lumber Selection

a. Choose wood species that are known for their stability and resistance to movement, particularly for projects that require precise fits or will be exposed to varying humidity levels.

b. When possible, select quarter-sawn or rift-sawn lumber, which tends to have a more consistent grain orientation and less tendency to warp or cup compared to plain-sawn lumber.

c. Look for lumber that has been properly kiln-dried to a moisture content appropriate for your region and intended use, typically between 6-12% for interior projects and 12-18% for exterior projects.

d. Allow the lumber to acclimate to your workshop environment for several days or weeks before cutting and assembly, to allow it to reach an equilibrium moisture content and minimize movement during construction.

4. Design and Construction Strategies

a. Use joinery techniques that allow for some degree of wood movement, such as elongated screw holes, sliding dovetails, or expansion slots, particularly when joining wood across the grain.

b. Avoid designs that restrict or constrain the natural movement of the wood, such as wide, unsupported spans or rigid, glued-up panels, which can lead to warping, splitting, or joint failure over time.

c. Incorporate elements that can help stabilize and reinforce the wood, such as cross-grain supports, braces, or frames, which can distribute stress and minimize deformation.

d. Consider using engineered wood products, such as plywood, MDF, or LVL, which are manufactured to be more dimensionally stable and less prone to movement than solid wood.

5. Finishing and Maintenance Practices

a. Apply finishes that can help seal and protect the wood from moisture infiltration and fluctuations, such as oil-based varnishes, lacquers, or water-resistant coatings.

b. Ensure that the finish is applied evenly and thoroughly, covering all surfaces and edges of the wood to create a consistent barrier against moisture.

c. Avoid exposing finished projects to extreme or rapid changes in humidity or temperature, such as placing them near heating vents, air conditioners, or windows with direct sunlight.

d. Regularly inspect and maintain finished projects, looking for signs of warping, splitting, or other damage, and address any issues promptly to prevent further deterioration.

6. Mitigation and Repair Techniques

a. If a piece of wood has already begun to warp or split, assess the severity and extent of the issue to determine the most appropriate course of action.

b. For minor warping, you may be able to correct the issue by applying moisture and pressure to the opposite side of the warp, using clamps, weights, or a moistened cloth, and allowing the wood to dry and reshape gradually.

c. For more severe warping or splitting, you may need to cut out and replace the affected section of wood, using joinery techniques that allow for movement and maintain the structural integrity of the piece.

d. In some cases, you may be able to stabilize or reinforce a warped or split piece of wood using epoxy, wood filler, or mechanical fasteners, such as screws, dowels, or butterfly keys, depending on the nature and location of the damage.

By understanding the causes and contributing factors of wood warping and splitting, and implementing appropriate prevention and mitigation strategies, you can minimize the occurrence and impact of these common issues in your woodworking projects. From selecting the right lumber and designing for movement to applying protective finishes and maintaining a stable environment, the key is to work with the natural characteristics of the wood and anticipate and accommodate its inherent tendencies. With knowledge, skill, and attention to detail, you can create woodworking projects that are both beautiful and durable, able to withstand the tests of time and the elements.

Correcting Staining and Finishing Issues

The process of staining and finishing wood is an essential aspect of many woodworking projects, as it enhances the natural beauty of the wood, protects it from damage, and creates a desired aesthetic. However, even with careful preparation and application, issues can arise during the staining and finishing process that may affect the final appearance and durability of the piece. In this section, we'll provide a detailed, structured, and in-depth explanation of common staining and finishing issues and the techniques for correcting them.

1. Identifying Staining and Finishing Issues

a. Uneven or Blotchy Stain: This occurs when the stain is absorbed inconsistently across the wood surface, resulting in darker or lighter patches or a mottled appearance.

b. Stain Not Adhering: If the stain appears to be sitting on top of the wood rather than absorbing into it, or if it can be easily wiped or scraped off, the stain may not be adhering properly.

c. Rough or Gritty Finish: A finish that feels rough, bumpy, or gritty to the touch may indicate issues with the application process, such as improper sanding, contamination, or incompatible products.

d. Bubbles or Foam in Finish: Small bubbles or foamy texture in the finish can be caused by over-brushing, shaking the can, or applying the finish too thickly or in humid conditions.

e. Brush Marks or Streaks: Visible brush strokes, lines, or streaks in the finish can result from using a low-quality brush, applying too much pressure, or not maintaining a wet edge during application.

f. Dust or Debris in Finish: Dust, hair, or other particles embedded in the finish can be caused by an unclean work environment, not allowing adequate drying time between coats, or not straining the finish before use.

2. Preparation and Prevention Techniques

a. Sand the wood surface thoroughly with progressively finer grits of sandpaper, starting with 80-120 grit and working up to 220-320 grit, to create a smooth, even surface for the stain and finish to adhere to.

b. Clean the wood surface with a tack cloth or vacuum to remove any dust, debris, or contaminants that may interfere with the stain or finish adhesion.

c. Test the stain and finish on a scrap piece of the same wood species to ensure compatibility, color accuracy, and desired results before applying to the main project.

d. Use pre-stain conditioners or wood sealers on woods prone to blotching, such as pine or cherry, to promote even stain absorption and minimize grain reversal.

e. Maintain a clean, dust-free work environment and use high-quality, clean brushes, rags, or spray equipment to apply the stain and finish, following the manufacturer's instructions for best results.

3. Correcting Uneven or Blotchy Stain

a. If the stain is still wet, try to even out the absorption by wiping the surface with a clean cloth or applying more stain to the lighter areas to match the darker areas.

b. If the stain has dried, you may need to sand the surface with fine-grit sandpaper (220-320 grit) to remove the uneven stain, then reapply the stain more consistently, using a pre-stain conditioner if necessary.

c. For severe cases of blotching, you may need to strip the stain completely using a chemical stripper or sanding, then re-sand and re-stain the surface, taking care to apply the stain evenly and wipe off any excess.

4. Addressing Stain Adhesion Issues

a. If the stain is not adhering properly, it may be due to a compatibility issue between the stain and the wood species or a previous finish on the wood. Strip any existing finishes and sand the surface thoroughly to create a clean, bare wood surface.

b. Ensure that the wood is dry and free of contaminants, such as oil, grease, or wax, which can prevent the stain from penetrating the wood fibers. Clean the surface with mineral spirits or a degreaser if necessary.

c. Apply a wood conditioner or sealer before staining to improve the stain's ability to adhere to the wood surface and create a more even color.

5. Fixing Rough or Gritty Finishes

a. If the finish feels rough or gritty, it may be due to improper sanding, contamination, or incompatible products. Sand the surface with fine-grit sandpaper (320-400 grit) to smooth out the texture.

b. Clean the surface thoroughly with a tack cloth or mineral spirits to remove any dust, debris, or contaminants that may be causing the rough texture.

c. Apply a compatible clear coat or topcoat over the existing finish to create a smoother, more even surface. Follow the manufacturer's instructions for application and drying times.

6. Removing Bubbles or Foam from Finishes

a. If bubbles or foam appear in the finish, try to brush them out gently with a clean, dry brush before the finish starts to dry.

b. If the bubbles have already dried, sand the surface with fine-grit sandpaper (320-400 grit) to pop and smooth out the bubbles, then reapply the finish in thinner, more even coats.

c. To prevent bubbles from forming, avoid shaking the finish can, over-brushing the surface, or applying the finish too thickly or in humid conditions. Use a quality brush and maintain a wet edge during application.

7. Eliminating Brush Marks or Streaks

a. If brush marks or streaks are visible in the finish, sand the surface lightly with fine-grit sandpaper (320-400 grit) to even out the texture.

b. Apply the finish in thinner, more even coats, using a high-quality brush and long, smooth strokes in the direction of the wood grain. Maintain a wet edge and avoid over-brushing the surface.

c. Consider using a foam brush, sprayer, or wiping cloth to apply the finish, which can help minimize brush marks and create a more even surface.

8. Removing Dust or Debris from Finishes

a. If dust or debris is embedded in the finish, allow the finish to dry completely, then sand the surface lightly with fine-grit sandpaper (320-400 grit) to remove the particles.

b. Clean the surface thoroughly with a tack cloth or compressed air to remove any sanding dust or debris before reapplying the finish.

c. To prevent dust or debris from settling in the finish, ensure that the work environment is clean and dust-free, and allow adequate drying time between coats. Strain the finish through a fine-mesh filter or cheesecloth before use.

By understanding the common issues that can arise during the staining and finishing process and the techniques for correcting them, you can achieve professional-quality results in your woodworking projects. Whether you're working with a new project or trying to salvage a piece with finishing flaws, the key is to approach the correction process systematically, using the appropriate methods and products for the specific issue at hand. With patience, skill, and attention to detail, you can overcome staining and finishing challenges and create woodworking pieces that showcase the natural beauty and durability of the wood.

Avoiding Measurement and Cutting Errors

Accurate measurements and precise cuts are essential for the success of any woodworking project. Errors in either of these areas can lead to ill-fitting joints, uneven surfaces, and overall dissatisfaction with the final product. In this section, we'll provide a detailed, structured, and in-depth explanation of common measurement and cutting errors and the strategies for avoiding them in your woodworking projects.

1. Understanding the Importance of Accuracy

a. Measurement accuracy: Precise measurements are crucial for ensuring that project components fit together correctly, align properly, and maintain the desired proportions and scale.

b. Cutting precision: Clean, accurate cuts are essential for creating tight-fitting joints, smooth surfaces, and visually appealing results. Imprecise cuts can lead to gaps, misalignments, and structural weaknesses.

c. Cumulative errors: Small measurement or cutting errors can compound throughout the project, leading to larger discrepancies and difficulties in assembly and finishing.

2. Common Measurement Errors and Solutions

a. Misreading or miscounting units: Carefully read and double-check measurements, paying attention to the specific units (inches, centimeters, etc.) and any fractions or decimals. Use a tape measure or ruler with clear, easy-to-read markings.

b. Incorrect transfer of measurements: When transferring measurements from plans or sketches to the workpiece, use a sharp pencil and a straight edge to ensure accuracy. Double-check the transferred measurements against the original dimensions.

c. Failure to account for blade thickness: When measuring for cuts, remember to account for the thickness of the saw blade (the kerf) to ensure that the final pieces are the correct size. Adjust measurements accordingly or use a blade with a thinner kerf.

d. Inconsistent measuring tools: Use the same measuring tool throughout the project to maintain consistency. Verify that the tool is accurate by comparing it against a known standard or a digital measuring device.

3. Strategies for Accurate Measuring

a. Use the appropriate measuring tool for the task: Select a measuring tool that is suitable for the size and precision of the measurement needed, such as a tape measure for larger dimensions or a combination square for smaller, more detailed measurements.

b. Calibrate and maintain measuring tools: Regularly check the accuracy of your measuring tools and calibrate them if necessary. Keep tools clean and stored properly to prevent damage or distortion.

c. Use story sticks or templates: Create physical reference pieces, such as story sticks or templates, to transfer measurements consistently and accurately across multiple components or projects.

d. Measure twice, cut once: Always double-check measurements before making cuts to avoid costly errors. Take the time to confirm dimensions, angles, and alignments before proceeding.

4. Common Cutting Errors and Solutions

a. Inaccurate cutting angles: Ensure that saw blades and cutting tools are set to the correct angle using a protractor, angle gauge, or digital angle finder. Use a miter gauge or fence to guide the workpiece and maintain a consistent angle during the cut.

b. Rough or splintered edges: Use sharp, high-quality saw blades appropriate for the type of wood and the desired cut. Support the workpiece adequately to minimize vibration and ensure a clean cut. Sand or trim rough edges as needed.

c. Wandering or veering cuts: Maintain a steady, controlled feed rate and keep the saw blade aligned with the cut line. Use guides, fences, or jigs to help steer the workpiece and prevent the blade from wandering.

d. Incorrect depth or width of cuts: Set the saw blade or cutting tool to the appropriate depth or width for the desired cut, using the tool's depth adjustment or a measured guide block. Test the setting on a scrap piece before cutting the final workpiece.

5. Techniques for Precise Cutting

a. Use marking tools for clear, accurate cut lines: Mark cut lines using a sharp pencil, marking knife, or marking gauge. Use a straight edge or square to ensure that lines are straight and perpendicular.

b. Employ cutting guides and jigs: Utilize cutting guides, jigs, or sleds to ensure consistent, accurate cuts, particularly for repetitive or complex cuts. These tools can help maintain the correct angle, depth, and position of the cut.

c. Make test cuts on scrap wood: Before cutting the final workpiece, make test cuts on scrap wood to verify the accuracy of measurements, angles, and tool settings. Adjust as needed based on the test results.

d. Cut incrementally and dry-fit components: When possible, cut components slightly larger than the final dimensions and gradually trim them down to the perfect fit. Dry-fit components together to check for proper alignment and make any necessary adjustments before final assembly.

6. Maintaining and Calibrating Cutting Tools

a. Keep saw blades and cutting tools sharp: Regularly sharpen or replace saw blades, router bits, and other cutting tools to ensure clean, precise cuts. Dull tools can cause tear-out, burning, or inaccurate cuts.

b. Check and adjust tool alignment: Periodically check the alignment of saw blades, fences, and miter gauges to ensure that they are square and true. Make necessary adjustments according to the manufacturer's instructions.

c. Clean and lubricate tools: Keep cutting tools clean and free of dust, pitch, or rust, which can affect their performance and accuracy. Lubricate moving parts as needed to ensure smooth, consistent operation.

7. Incorporating Patience and Planning

a. Take your time: Rushing through measurements and cuts can lead to errors and inaccuracies. Work at a steady, deliberate pace, focusing on precision and quality rather than speed.

b. Double-check your work: After making measurements and cuts, take a moment to double-check the results against the plans or intended dimensions. Verify that components fit together correctly and make any necessary adjustments before proceeding.

c. Plan and organize your work: Before beginning a project, take the time to plan out the sequence of measurements and cuts, ensuring that you have all the necessary tools and materials on hand. Keep your work area clean and organized to minimize distractions and errors.

By understanding the common measurement and cutting errors and employing the strategies and techniques outlined above, you can significantly improve the accuracy and precision of your woodworking projects. Remember that achieving perfect results takes practice, patience, and a commitment to continuous improvement. As you gain experience and refine your skills, you'll develop a keen eye for detail and a steady hand that will help you create stunning, precise woodworking pieces.

Chapter 9
Resources and Further Learning
Recommended Tools and Brands

As you embark on your woodwórking journey, having the right tools and resources can make a significant difference in the quality of your work and your overall enjoyment of the craft. In this section, we'll provide a detailed, structured, and in-depth look at recommended tools and brands to help you make informed decisions when equipping your workshop and expanding your knowledge.

1. Essential Hand Tools
a. Chisels
- Recommended brands: Lie-Nielsen, Veritas, Stanley Sweetheart, Narex
- Look for high-quality steel, comfortable handles, and a range of sizes (e.g., 1/4", 1/2", 3/4", 1")

b. Hand Planes
- Recommended brands: Lie-Nielsen, Veritas, Stanley Bedrock, Wood River
- Essential planes include a block plane, a jack plane, and a smoothing plane

c. Hand Saws
- Recommended brands: Lie-Nielsen, Veritas, Bad Axe, Florip
- Consider a dovetail saw, a tenon saw, and a carcass saw for various joinery tasks

d. Marking and Measuring Tools
- Recommended brands: Starrett, Mitutoyo, iGaging, Woodpeckers
- Invest in a good combination square, marking gauge, and set of calipers

2. Power Tools

a. Table Saw
- Recommended brands: SawStop, Powermatic, Jet, Grizzly
- Look for a sturdy, cast-iron top, a powerful motor, and good dust collection

b. Bandsaw
- Recommended brands: Laguna, Rikon, Jet, Grizzly
- Consider a 14" or larger model with a strong motor and good blade guides

c. Router
- Recommended brands: Festool, Porter-Cable, Bosch, DeWalt
- Choose a plunge router or a fixed-base router with variable speed control

d. Drill Press
- Recommended brands: Jet, Delta, Rikon, Wen
- Look for a model with a good depth stop, a large table, and variable speed settings

3. Sharpening and Maintenance Tools

a. Sharpening Stones
- Recommended brands: Norton, Shapton, DMT, King
- Invest in a set of water stones or diamond stones for sharpening chisels and plane irons

b. Honing Guide
- Recommended brands: Veritas, Lie-Nielsen, Eclipse
- A honing guide helps maintain consistent bevel angles when sharpening

c. Blade Cleaning and Conditioning
- Recommended brands: Bostik GlideCote, Boshield T-9, Jojoba Oil
- Regular cleaning and conditioning of blades helps prevent rust and improves performance

4. Workbench and Vises

a. Workbench Designs
- Recommended styles: Roubo, Nicholson, Moravian, Scandinavian
- Choose a design that suits your space, budget, and woodworking style

b. Vises
- Recommended brands: Benchcrafted, Veritas, Wilton, Yost
- Consider a face vise, tail vise, or leg vise for versatile workholding options

5. Safety Equipment

a. Ear Protection
- Recommended brands: 3M, Howard Leight, Peltor
- Look for comfortable, adjustable earmuffs or earplugs with a high NRR (Noise Reduction Rating)

b. Eye Protection
- Recommended brands: Uvex, 3M, DeWalt, Oakley
- Choose safety glasses or goggles with impact resistance and a comfortable fit

c. Respiratory Protection
- Recommended brands: 3M, North Safety, Gerson, Elipse
- Use a dust mask or respirator when sanding, cutting, or working with finishes

6. Educational Resources

a. Books
- "The Anarchist's Toolchest" by Christopher Schwarz
- "Understanding Wood Finishing" by Bob Flexner
- "The Complete Illustrated Guide to Joinery" by Gary Rogowski
- "The Essential Woodworker" by Robert Wearing

b. Online Courses and Videos
- Paul Sellers' Woodworking Masterclasses
- The Wood Whisperer by Marc Spagnuolo
- Fine Woodworking's Video Workshop Series
- Rob Cosman's YouTube Channel

c. Magazines and Websites
- Fine Woodworking
- Popular Woodworking
- Woodsmith
- LumberJocks.com

7. Woodworking Communities

a. Local Guilds and Clubs
- Search for woodworking guilds, clubs, or maker spaces in your area
- Attend meetings, workshops, and events to connect with fellow woodworkers

b. Online Forums and Groups
- Woodnet.net
- Sawmill Creek
- WoodworkingTalk.com
- Reddit's r/woodworking community

c. Social Media
- Follow woodworking hashtags on Instagram, such as #woodworking, #handtools, and #workbench
- Join Facebook groups dedicated to specific aspects of woodworking, like hand tool users or furniture makers

By investing in quality tools from reputable brands and taking advantage of the wealth of educational resources and supportive communities available, you can accelerate your growth as a woodworker and gain the knowledge and skills needed to create exceptional pieces. Remember that building a tool collection and a knowledge base takes time, so focus on acquiring the most essential tools and resources first, and then expand your arsenal as your interests and needs evolve.

As you explore the recommended tools and brands, take the time to read reviews, compare features, and consider your specific needs and budget. Don't be afraid to ask questions or seek advice from more experienced woodworkers, as they can offer valuable insights and help you make informed decisions.

Finally, remember that the most important tool in your workshop is your own curiosity, dedication, and willingness to learn. Embrace the challenges and opportunities that woodworking presents, and enjoy the journey of developing your skills and creating beautiful, functional pieces that will last a lifetime.

Online Woodworking Communities and Forums

In the digital age, online woodworking communities and forums have become invaluable resources for woodworkers of all skill levels. These virtual spaces provide a platform for sharing knowledge, seeking advice, showcasing projects, and connecting with like-minded individuals who share a passion for the craft. In this section, we'll take a detailed, structured, and in-depth look at the benefits of participating in online woodworking communities and forums, as well as some popular platforms to explore.

1. Benefits of Online Woodworking Communities
  a. Knowledge Sharing
- Access a wealth of information, tips, and techniques shared by experienced woodworkers
- Learn about new tools, materials, and methods from a diverse group of craftspeople
- Get feedback and advice on your projects, designs, and ideas
  b. Inspiration and Motivation
- Discover inspiring projects and designs shared by other community members
- Find motivation to tackle new challenges and push your skills to the next level
- Participate in community challenges, contests, or themed projects to spark creativity
  c. Troubleshooting and Problem-Solving
- Get help diagnosing and resolving issues with your tools, techniques, or projects
- Benefit from the collective knowledge and experience of the community
- Find solutions to common problems or discover alternative approaches

d. Camaraderie and Support
- Connect with fellow woodworkers who share your passion and interests
- Engage in discussions, debates, and friendly banter about all things woodworking
- Receive encouragement and support from a community that understands the joys and challenges of the craft

2. Popular Woodworking Forums
a. Lumberjocks.com
- One of the largest and most active woodworking communities online
- Features project galleries, forums, blogs, and reviews
- Covers a wide range of woodworking topics, from beginner to advanced
- Offers a friendly and supportive atmosphere for woodworkers of all skill levels

b. Woodworking Talk
- A vibrant community with active forums covering various aspects of woodworking
- Includes sections for project showcases, tool discussions, and technique sharing
- Provides a welcoming environment for asking questions and seeking advice
- Features a marketplace for buying, selling, or trading tools and materials

c. Sawmill Creek Woodworking Community
- A long-standing forum with a focus on traditional woodworking and craftsmanship
- Covers topics such as hand tools, joinery, furniture making, and finishing
- Offers a wealth of knowledge from experienced woodworkers and professionals
- Provides a respectful and helpful community atmosphere

d. WoodNet Forums
- A comprehensive forum covering a broad range of woodworking topics
- Includes sections for general woodworking, turning, carving, and scrolling
- Features active discussions on tools, techniques, and project planning
- Offers a mix of hobbyist and professional perspectives and insights

3. Specialty Woodworking Forums
a. Scrollsaw Village
- A dedicated forum for scrollsaw enthusiasts and artists
- Covers various aspects of scrollsaw technique, pattern design, and project ideas
- Offers a supportive community for sharing work, asking questions, and providing feedback

b. American Association of Woodturners (AAW) Forum
- The official forum of the AAW, a leading organization for woodturning enthusiasts
- Covers all aspects of woodturning, from beginner to advanced techniques
- Provides access to expert advice, project ideas, and event information
- Offers a community focused on promoting and advancing the art and craft of woodturning

c. Woodcarving Illustrated Forum
- A forum dedicated to the art and craft of woodcarving
- Covers various styles and techniques, from whittling to relief carving
- Provides a platform for sharing projects, patterns, and tips
- Offers a supportive community for carvers of all skill levels

4. Getting the Most Out of Online Woodworking Communities

a. Introduce Yourself

- Take a moment to introduce yourself to the community and share your woodworking background and interests
- Engage in "new member" or "introduction" threads to connect with other newcomers and established members

b. Read the Rules and Guidelines

- Familiarize yourself with the forum's rules, guidelines, and etiquette expectations
- Understand the community's norms and conventions for posting, responding, and interacting

c. Use the Search Function

- Before posting a question or starting a new thread, use the forum's search function to see if your topic has been discussed before
- Explore existing threads and resources to find answers and insights related to your interests

d. Participate Actively

- Engage in discussions, ask questions, and share your thoughts and experiences
- Offer advice, feedback, and encouragement to other community members
- Contribute to the community by sharing your projects, techniques, and lessons learned

e. Be Respectful and Open-minded

- Treat other community members with respect and courtesy, even if you disagree with their opinions or approaches
- Be open to different perspectives and ideas, and appreciate the diversity of skills and backgrounds within the community

f. Give Back to the Community

- As you grow and develop your skills, look for opportunities to help and support other woodworkers
- Share your knowledge, experiences, and resources to contribute to the collective wisdom of the community

- Participate in community events, challenges, or initiatives to foster a sense of collaboration and camaraderie

By actively participating in online woodworking communities and forums, you can tap into a vast network of knowledge, inspiration, and support. These platforms provide an invaluable opportunity to learn from experienced craftspeople, share your own insights and experiences, and connect with fellow woodworkers who share your passion for the craft.

As you explore different communities and forums, take the time to observe the unique culture, tone, and focus of each platform. Some forums may be more geared toward specific aspects of woodworking, such as hand tools, turning, or carving, while others may have a broader scope. Find the communities that align with your interests and goals, and engage actively to get the most out of your participation.

Remember that online communities are built on a foundation of mutual respect, collaboration, and a shared love for woodworking. By contributing positively to these communities and being open to learning from others, you can not only enhance your own woodworking journey but also help to enrich the experiences of your fellow craftspeople.

Woodworking Classes and Workshops

Attending woodworking classes and workshops is an excellent way to develop your skills, learn new techniques, and gain hands-on experience under the guidance of experienced instructors. Whether you're a beginner looking to establish a strong foundation or an experienced woodworker seeking to refine your craft, participating in structured learning opportunities can provide valuable insights and accelerate your growth. In this section, we'll explore the benefits of woodworking classes and workshops, the types of programs available, and tips for finding and making the most of these educational experiences.

1. Benefits of Woodworking Classes and Workshops
a. Structured Learning
- Follow a well-designed curriculum that progressively builds skills and knowledge
- Benefit from a logical sequence of lessons that cover techniques, tools, and materials
- Receive clear explanations, demonstrations, and feedback from knowledgeable instructors

b. Hands-on Experience
- Gain practical experience working with tools, machines, and materials
- Apply techniques and concepts under the guidance of skilled instructors
- Develop muscle memory, dexterity, and confidence through hands-on practice

c. Personalized Instruction
- Receive individual attention and feedback from instructors
- Get answers to your specific questions and guidance tailored to your skill level
- Benefit from real-time corrections, adjustments, and advice to refine your technique

d. Inspiration and Motivation
- Immerse yourself in a creative and supportive learning environment
- Draw inspiration from the projects, ideas, and achievements of your classmates
- Stay motivated and accountable through the structure and expectations of the program

2. Types of Woodworking Classes and Workshops
a. Beginner Classes
- Ideal for those new to woodworking or looking to build a strong foundation
- Cover essential tools, techniques, and safety procedures
- Typically focus on basic projects like boxes, cutting boards, or simple furniture

b. Intermediate and Advanced Classes
- Suitable for woodworkers with some experience and a grasp of fundamental skills
- Explore more complex techniques, specialized tools, and advanced joinery methods
- Often focus on specific projects or skill sets, such as cabinetmaking, veneering, or carving

c. Specialized Workshops
- Focused on specific aspects of woodworking, such as turning, carving, or marquetry
- Provide in-depth instruction and hands-on experience in a particular area of interest
- Often led by renowned experts or master craftspeople in their respective fields

d. Project-based Classes
- Centered around completing a specific project, such as a piece of furniture or a decorative item
- Provide step-by-step guidance and skill-building opportunities throughout the project

- Allow participants to create a tangible product while learning new techniques and concepts

3. Finding Woodworking Classes and Workshops
a. Local Woodworking Schools
- Search for dedicated woodworking schools or training programs in your area
- Look for institutions that offer structured curricula and experienced instructors
- Consider factors such as location, schedule, and tuition costs when evaluating options

b. Community Colleges and Adult Education Programs
- Check if local community colleges or adult education centers offer woodworking classes
- These programs often provide affordable access to tools, materials, and instruction
- Look for classes that align with your skill level and learning goals

c. Woodworking Stores and Suppliers
- Inquire if local woodworking stores or suppliers offer classes or workshops
- These programs may be focused on specific tools, techniques, or products
- Take advantage of the expertise and resources available through these retailers

d. Online Platforms and Resources
- Explore online learning platforms, such as Craftsy or Skillshare, for woodworking courses
- Consider enrolling in online workshops or video-based lessons from experienced instructors
- Benefit from the flexibility and convenience of learning at your own pace and schedule

4. Preparing for a Woodworking Class or Workshop

a. Review the Course Description and Requirements

- Carefully read the course description, objectives, and prerequisites
- Ensure that the class aligns with your skill level and learning goals
- Confirm that you meet any requirements for tools, materials, or prior experience

b. Gather Necessary Tools and Materials

- Check if the class or workshop provides tools and materials or if you need to bring your own
- Invest in quality tools and materials that will support your learning and long-term woodworking goals
- Ensure that your tools are sharp, properly maintained, and ready for use

c. Familiarize Yourself with Safety Procedures

- Review basic woodworking safety guidelines and best practices
- Familiarize yourself with the proper use and maintenance of personal protective equipment
- Understand the safety features and procedures for any tools or machines you'll be using

d. Set Personal Learning Goals

- Identify specific skills, techniques, or concepts you want to focus on during the class
- Consider how the class fits into your overall woodworking learning journey
- Set realistic goals for what you hope to achieve and take away from the experience

5. Making the Most of Your Woodworking Class or Workshop Experience

a. Engage Actively in the Learning Process

- Participate fully in lectures, demonstrations, and hands-on activities

- Ask questions and seek clarification when needed to deepen your understanding
- Take notes, make sketches, and document your learning for future reference

b. Practice and Apply What You Learn

- Take advantage of in-class opportunities to practice new techniques and skills
- Apply the concepts and methods you learn to your own projects and experiments
- Seek feedback and guidance from instructors to refine your technique and troubleshoot issues

c. Collaborate and Learn from Your Peers

- Engage with your classmates and learn from their experiences, ideas, and perspectives
- Offer support, encouragement, and constructive feedback to create a positive learning environment
- Participate in group projects or discussions to expand your understanding and skills

d. Continue Your Learning Journey

- Reflect on what you learned and identify areas for further growth and development
- Apply your new skills and knowledge to personal projects and continue practicing
- Seek additional learning opportunities, such as advanced classes or self-directed study, to build upon your foundation

By embracing the opportunities provided by woodworking classes and workshops, you can accelerate your growth as a craftsperson and unlock new levels of skill, creativity, and satisfaction in your woodworking journey. Whether you're a beginner seeking a strong foundation or an experienced woodworker looking to master new techniques, structured learning experiences offer a wealth of benefits and opportunities for personal and professional development.

As you explore the world of woodworking education, remember to approach each class or workshop with an open mind, a willingness to learn, and a commitment to active participation. Embrace the challenges and opportunities that come with stepping outside your comfort zone, and trust in the guidance and expertise of your instructors and peers.

By combining the knowledge and skills gained through woodworking classes and workshops with your own dedication, practice, and creativity, you can achieve your woodworking goals and unlock your full potential as a craftsperson. Embrace the lifelong journey of learning and growth, and let your passion for woodworking guide you to new heights of mastery and satisfaction.

Inspiration and Ideas for Future Projects

As you continue to develop your woodworking skills and knowledge, it's essential to keep your creative spark alive by seeking out inspiration and ideas for future projects. By exploring a wide range of sources and styles, you can expand your horizons, challenge yourself to try new techniques, and discover exciting possibilities for expressing your unique vision and craftsmanship. In this section, we'll delve into various methods for finding inspiration and generating ideas for your future woodworking projects, providing a detailed, structured, and in-depth look at the creative process.

1. Exploring Woodworking Styles and Traditions
a. Traditional and Classic Styles
- Investigate classic woodworking styles such as Shaker, Arts and Crafts, or Queen Anne
- Study the key elements, proportions, and details that define each style
- Consider how you can incorporate traditional techniques or design principles into your projects

b. Contemporary and Modern Styles
- Explore contemporary woodworking styles that emphasize clean lines, minimalism, and functionality
- Study the work of modern woodworkers and designers to understand current trends and innovations
- Consider how you can infuse your projects with a fresh, modern aesthetic while respecting tradition

c. Cultural and Regional Influences
- Research woodworking traditions from different cultures and regions around the world
- Explore the unique materials, techniques, and design elements that characterize each tradition
- Consider how you can incorporate cultural influences or regional materials into your projects

2. Analyzing Inspirational Projects and Pieces

a. Studying Masterworks and Iconic Designs

- Examine the work of renowned woodworkers, furniture makers, and designers throughout history
- Analyze the forms, proportions, joinery, and decorative elements that make each piece exceptional
- Consider how you can adapt or interpret the principles and techniques of these masterworks in your own projects

b. Deconstructing Project Designs

- Select a project or piece that inspires you and break down its components and construction methods
- Study the materials, joinery, and finishing techniques used to create the piece
- Consider how you can modify, simplify, or elaborate on the design to suit your skills and preferences

c. Identifying Design Elements and Principles

- Examine the aesthetic qualities and design principles that make a project visually appealing and harmonious
- Study the use of line, form, proportion, balance, contrast, and repetition in successful designs
- Consider how you can apply these design elements and principles to create cohesive and impactful projects

3. Seeking Inspiration Beyond Woodworking

a. Exploring Other Craft Disciplines

- Study the techniques, materials, and aesthetics of related craft disciplines such as metalworking, ceramics, or textiles
- Consider how you can incorporate elements or principles from these disciplines into your woodworking projects
- Explore the potential for collaborative or multi-disciplinary projects that combine woodworking with other crafts

b. Drawing from Nature and the Environment

- Observe the forms, patterns, and textures found in nature and consider how they can inspire your designs

- Study the properties and characteristics of different wood species and how they can be showcased in your projects
- Consider how you can incorporate sustainable or locally-sourced materials into your work

c. Finding Inspiration in Everyday Objects and Experiences
- Look for design inspiration in the objects, architecture, and experiences that surround you daily
- Consider how the function, form, and aesthetics of everyday items can be translated into woodworking projects
- Reflect on your personal experiences, memories, and emotions and how they can inform your creative vision

4. Engaging with the Woodworking Community

a. Attending Woodworking Shows and Exhibitions
- Visit woodworking shows, exhibitions, and galleries to see the latest trends, techniques, and innovations
- Engage with exhibitors, makers, and attendees to learn about their projects, processes, and inspirations
- Consider how the work you encounter can inspire and inform your own creative journey

b. Participating in Woodworking Clubs and Guilds
- Join a local woodworking club or guild to connect with fellow enthusiasts and learn from their experiences
- Participate in group projects, challenges, or exhibitions to stretch your skills and explore new ideas
- Consider how the feedback, support, and camaraderie of a woodworking community can enrich your creative process

c. Engaging with Online Woodworking Platforms and Social Media
- Follow woodworking hashtags, accounts, and pages on social media platforms to discover new makers and projects
- Participate in online woodworking forums, groups, and communities to share ideas and get feedback on your work
- Consider how the global reach and diversity of online woodworking platforms can expand your creative horizons

5. Developing and Refining Project Ideas

a. Brainstorming and Mind Mapping

- Use brainstorming techniques, such as mind mapping or free association, to generate a wide range of project ideas
- Explore the connections and relationships between different ideas and consider how they can be combined or developed
- Refine your ideas by evaluating their feasibility, originality, and alignment with your skills and interests

b. Sketching and Prototyping

- Use sketching and drawing to visualize and refine your project ideas, exploring different forms, proportions, and details
- Create small-scale models or prototypes to test the functionality and aesthetics of your designs
- Consider how the process of sketching and prototyping can help you identify and solve potential challenges or limitations

c. Planning and Executing Projects

- Develop detailed plans, drawings, and cut lists for your chosen project ideas
- Source the necessary materials, tools, and resources to bring your ideas to life
- Execute your projects with care, precision, and attention to detail, allowing for flexibility and adaptation as needed

By actively seeking inspiration and ideas for future projects, you can fuel your creativity, expand your skills, and push the boundaries of your woodworking practice. Whether you draw inspiration from traditional styles, contemporary innovations, or cross-disciplinary influences, the key is to remain open, curious, and engaged in the creative process.

As you explore different sources of inspiration and generate new project ideas, remember to balance creativity with practicality, considering factors such as your skill level, available resources, and intended use or audience for each piece. Don't be afraid to take risks, experiment with new techniques or materials, and learn from both successes and challenges along the way.

Ultimately, the most inspiring and successful woodworking projects are those that reflect your unique voice, vision, and passion as a maker. By staying true to your creative instincts, continually refining your skills and knowledge, and embracing the endless possibilities of woodworking, you can create pieces that not only showcase your technical prowess but also tell a story and evoke an emotional response in those who encounter them.

So, keep exploring, keep creating, and keep pushing the boundaries of what's possible in your woodworking journey. With dedication, perseverance, and a never-ending quest for inspiration and growth, you can build a rich and rewarding creative practice that brings joy, fulfillment, and beauty to your life and the lives of those around you.

Conclusion

As we conclude our exploration of the world of woodworking and carpentry, it's clear that this craft is more than just a set of skills or techniques – it's a way of life, a creative outlet, and a means of self-expression. Throughout this book, we've delved into the many facets of woodworking, from the fundamentals of tools and materials to the intricacies of advanced joinery and finishing techniques. We've explored the joys and challenges of tackling projects big and small, from simple shelves and cutting boards to complex pieces of furniture and cabinetry.

But beyond the technical knowledge and practical tips, what emerges is a sense of the deep satisfaction and personal growth that comes from creating something beautiful and functional with your own hands. Woodworking is a craft that demands patience, perseverance, and attention to detail, but it also rewards us with a profound sense of accomplishment and pride in our work.

As you embark on your own woodworking journey, remember that the key to success lies not just in mastering the skills and techniques, but in cultivating a mindset of curiosity, creativity, and continuous learning. Embrace the challenges and opportunities that come with each project, and don't be afraid to make mistakes, experiment with new ideas, and push the boundaries of your comfort zone.

Draw inspiration from the rich history and traditions of woodworking, but also look to the future and the endless possibilities that new technologies, materials, and design innovations offer. Engage with the vibrant and supportive community of woodworkers around the world, sharing your knowledge, experiences, and passion with others who share your love for this timeless craft.

Above all, remember that woodworking is a journey, not a destination. It's a lifelong pursuit of mastery, creativity, and self-discovery, one that can bring joy, fulfillment, and beauty to every aspect of your life. So, as you close the pages of this book and step into your workshop, do so with a sense of excitement, curiosity, and openness to the endless possibilities that await you.

May your tools be sharp, your wood be true, and your creativity flow freely as you craft a life and a legacy through the timeless art of woodworking. Happy building!

Manufactured by Amazon.ca
Bolton, ON

41528630R00098